Published by John Wiley & Sons, Inc., Hoboken, New Jersey
Published simultaneously in Canada

Design and production by Navta Associates, Inc.

For general information about our other products and services, please contact our Customer Care Department within the United States at (800) 762-2974, outside the United States at (317) 572-3993 or fax (317) 572-4002.

Wiley also publishes its books in a variety of electronic formats. Some content that appears in print may not be available in electronic books.

ISBN 0-471-21189-3

Printed in the United States of America

10 9 8 7 6 5 4 3 2 1

Columbus
in the Americas

WILLIAM LEAST
HEAT-MOON

John Wiley & Sons, Inc.

This little book is for
Mary Barile, Jack LaZebnik,
Chris Walker

Contents

Prologue

Of the four crossings Christopher Columbus made to the Americas between his first departure in August 1492 and the return from his final voyage in November 1504, we know, happily, the most about the initial trip and its opening of the Americas to Europe. In fact, we know assuredly more about those 224 days of the original exploration than we do about the first four decades of his life.

Still, we could have learned even more had not the manuscript of his 1492–93 logbook and a subsequent copy of it both disappeared within fifty years of his death. Upon his return to Spain, Columbus went to Seville to report to King Ferdinand and Queen Isabella the results of what he called "the Enterprise of the Indies." He gave to the Sovereigns his *Diario de a Bordo (The Outboard Log)* which the Queen had a scribe make an exact copy of for the newly proclaimed Admiral of the Ocean Sea. Those last two words are not a tautology but the prevailing name of the Atlantic, half of it then unknown. Columbus received the transcription six months later, just before leaving on his Second Voyage. The original has not been seen since Isabella's death in 1504. When the explorer died two years later, the duplicate passed into his family where it also soon vanished. Today, we have only a slender hope that either the original logbook or its copy might some day come again to light.

Before the transcription disappeared, Bartolomé de Las Casas, a Dominican friar and historian who knew both Columbus and the Caribbean world, borrowed the duplicate long enough to make his own version which in places quotes directly from the *Diario* and in others is merely a summation of daily entries. The one for the second day of the First Voyage, for example, in its entirety is this: "They went southwest by south." Fortunately, when Columbus reaches the Caribbean, Las Casas allows the entries to become longer and richer, often quoting its author to give details describing explorations among the islands.

The Las Casas rendition of the logbook is largely an abstract. Nevertheless, the most authoritative translation in English to date—the one of Oliver Dunn and James E. Kelley—requires nearly two hundred pages; we can assume what Columbus gave the Queen was a lengthy work indeed and, surely, for its own time and for many years to come, a nautical journal of unequaled fullness. In the long preface to his logbook, Columbus says he intends to record "very diligently" all that he will see and experience, so the loss of most of his own words is incalculable. Even in its abstracted state, we can fairly consider the *Diario* as one of the last grand documents of the Middle Ages and the first of a renaissance the Western Hemisphere would help generate in Europe.

The standard elements in a ship's log are usually present: headings, speed, distance covered, wind direction, sea conditions, damage reports, and so forth. While these details may be of slight interest to many readers, they are important for the interpretation and reconstruction of just where and how Columbus and his men sailed, but we should realize that after five centuries, despite much research in the last couple of hundred years, we must make many assumptions, some of them still, and probably forever, highly debatable.

A few other sources help fill in gaps or reinforce interpretations of the log as they also give crucial information on the subsequent voyages. The monumental opus of Las Casas, his *Historia de las Indies (History of the Indies)*—a work, surprisingly, never fully translated into English—contains numerous additional details as does the biography of Columbus that his learned second son, Ferdinand, wrote. Two other sixteenth-century scholars also help flesh out the explorations: Gonzalo Fernández de Oviedo's natural history of the Caribbean *(Historia General y Natural de las Indias)* complements Las Casas, and the

Italian Peter Martyr's account of the European opening of the New World—a term he popularized—*De Rebus Oceanicis et Orbe Novo*. From Columbus himself, we also have "the Barcelona Letter" of 1493 which concisely describes the First Voyage. Finally, we can draw upon four of the books Columbus owned, three of them replete with his annotations elaborating his geographical notions and his long belief that a ship could reach the Far East by sailing west.

In *Columbus in the Americas,* I have assembled his story from the explorer's own words and these secondary sources, as well as from selected modern research and interpretations acknowledged sound by most contemporary historians. It is not the purpose of this small book to address the many controversies that surround Christopher Columbus. Everywhere, I have tried to remain within the facts enjoying the broadest acceptance so that readers may see who Columbus was and comprehend much of what he did and was attempting to do. My hope is that solid history will replace popular myths about the man who did not discover America but surely did open it, for better and for worse, to a substantial remaking. His is a story of high adventure and deep darkness.

The First Voyage

---

one

The stillness of that predawn Friday belied what was about to transpire. On August the third, the Tinto River, lying as unruffled as the air, gave no suggestion that the world was about to be remade—deeply, widely, powerfully, and at times violently. Every beginning has a thousand beginnings and those beginnings have a thousand more, so that all inceptions carry unnumbered antecedents. To say of anything, "At that moment and in that place, it all began," is shortsighted, but within such shortsightedness, the European remaking of America and the American remaking of Europe began on a sluggish and undistinguished Spanish river near the commensurately undistinguished town of Palos not far from the Portuguese border. The King of Portugal, the greatest sea-faring nation of the day, had turned down an expedition like the one of three ships about to catch the

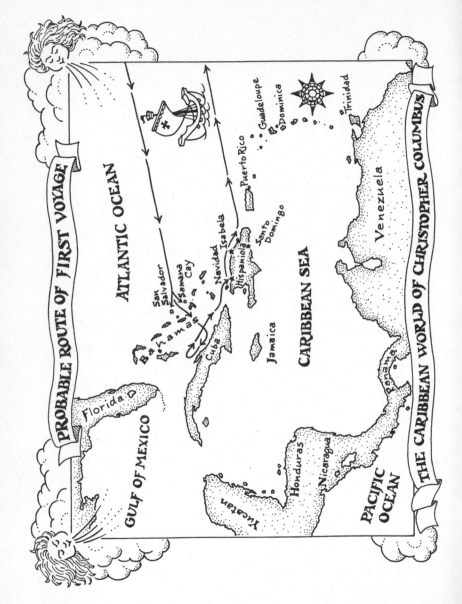

PROBABLE ROUTE OF FIRST VOYAGE

THE CARIBBEAN WORLD OF CHRISTOPHER COLUMBUS

ATLANTIC OCEAN

GULF OF MEXICO

CARIBBEAN SEA

PACIFIC OCEAN

Florida

San Salvador

Samana Cay

Bahamas

Cuba

Navidad

Isabela

Hispaniola

Santo Domingo

Puerto Rico

Guadeloupe

Dominica

Trinidad

Venezuela

Jamaica

Yucatan

Honduras

Nicaragua

Panama

tide half an hour before the summer sunrise and be pulled toward the sea.

Christopher Columbus, the Captain General of the fleet, took communion in a chapel nearby before boarding his flagship and, "in the name of Jesus," giving the command to weigh anchors of the wooden vessels, small even by the standards of 1492. The seamen, perhaps taking up a chantey appropriate to the task, leaned into the long oars, stirred the polished river surface, and began moving the ships laden with enough provisions to last several months. Under the limp sails, to the groan of timbers and the creak of oars, ninety men began a voyage to an unforeseen but not unimagined land across uncharted waters in hopes of finding an unproved route to an Asian civilization more ancient than the one they were leaving. What the sailors didn't know was that they were headed to a soon-to-be-dubbed New World inhabited by peoples whose ancestors had resided there for at least 25,000 years. Even more significantly, the mariners were the small vanguard that would open not only a place new to them but also a new era that would slowly and occasionally catastrophically reach the entire planet. Those few sailors were initiating blindly but with highly materialistic motives new conceptions of civilization. Pulling on the oars, the able seamen had scarcely a notion they were propelling themselves and everyone to come after them into a new realm that would redefine what it means to be human.

When *Santa María, Pinta,* and *Niña* crossed the sandy bar to enter the Atlantic Ocean about a hundred miles west of the Strait of Gibraltar, it was eight o'clock in the morning. Sea wind inflated the slack sails and forced a due southerly bearing the fleet followed until after sundown when the commander altered his course for the Canary Islands. The entire first day the men could look over the rails to see shoreline, but when they awoke the next morning, land was beyond anyone's ken.

Christopher Columbus—born Cristoforo Colombo but called in Spain Cristóbal Colón—was above average height (that still could mean under six feet), ruddy of face, aquiline nose, blue eyes, freckled, his reddish hair going white although he was only days away from his forty-second birthday. He was an experienced seaman, an excellent navigator with a scholarly bent and a devotion to his religion. We have his appearance from descriptions written by people who met him rather than from any pictures made during his life, for none has survived; given the time, that isn't surprising—portraits of even wealthy people were not common.

Although facts are scant, we do know with enough assurance to discount claims otherwise that he was born in northern Italy near Genoa, a major seaport, to Christian parents sometime between August 25 and October 31, 1451. His father was a master weaver and his mother the daughter of a weaver; Christopher and his younger brother, Bartholomew, also briefly worked in the woolen trade. Neither boy had much, if any, formal schooling. Christopher read classic geographical accounts in Latin, and he later learned to speak Portuguese and Spanish. His youth was not impoverished, and his days in Genoa apparently were happy enough to allow him to honor that city throughout his life.

Columbus grew up in a medieval world exhausted by war and bigotries, religious corruption and intolerance, a time of widespread spiritual disillusion and social pessimism, a continent deeply in need of a rebirth. The very day before his little fleet departed Palos, the last ships holding Jews who refused to convert to Christianity were by royal edict to leave port for exile in the Levant. If Columbus, who must have witnessed this hellish expulsion as he readied his crews and vessels, was moved by the cruelty of the decree, he left no mention of it other than a general phrase, absent of any judgment, in the preamble to his log. His last act on European soil—his confession of sins—we may reasonably assume did not include anything about the boatloads of misery that had weighed anchor only hours before. This is not irrelevant contemporary moralizing, because the new realms he was about to force open would eventually give a poisoned Old World new opportunities to create several societies where such inquisitions and purges, tortures and pogroms, eventually would become all but impossible, and nations he never dreamed of would offer new lives to descendants of people Ferdinand and Isabella were expelling. Of several indirect and unintended Columbian contributions to humankind, this is one.

two

The first forty-eight hours of Columbus on the open Atlantic exist today as a mere two sentences telling nothing more than bearings and distances, but on the sixth of August the first accident occurred: The large rudder of *Pinta* jumped its gudgeons, that is, broke loose from its fastenings. Because of a rough sea, Columbus could bring *Santa María* only close enough to offer encouragement to the resourceful and independent captain of the *Pinta,* Martín Alonso Pinzón, and trust he would find a way to jury-rig the rudder. Pinzón succeeded in a temporary repair, and Columbus praised him for his ingenuity, a compliment not to be repeated for reasons that will become evident. Pinzón believed the problem was not an accident but the work of the owner of the caravel, who was also aboard and allegedly unhappy at having his ship by royal order commandeered for the expedition. Given the capacity of the Atlantic in those waters to beat up small vessels, and given the stupidity of endangering the very ship one is aboard, Pinzón's assertion seems dubious. Although Columbus himself had to charter his flagship *Santa María,* Ferdinand and Isabella granted him temporary use of the two other ships from Palos for a municipal offense the town committed against the crown.

On the morning of August the ninth, the sailors could see Grand Canary Island, but a calm prevented them from reaching harbor. After three days, a breeze rose and moved the ships into the isles, with the limping *Pinta* heading to Las Palmas while the other ships sailed farther west to pass under the smoking volcano on Tenerife and anchor at San Sebastián on Gomera, one of the western Canaries. Despite the calm, the voyage from Palos had taken just twelve days, but waiting for repairs to *Pinta* required the next three and a half weeks. Columbus used the forced layover in the islands to change the triangular sails of *Niña* to square ones similar to those of her sister ships, a modification that also lessened the dangerous task of handling unwieldy canvas sheets at sea. The crews brought new supplies aboard, particularly food, water, and firewood. In effect, the first leg of the voyage, Palos to the Canaries, served as a shakedown cruise for an expedition put together rather hurriedly.

While on Gomera, Columbus may have been smitten by their beautiful governor, Doña Beatriz de Peraza y Bobadilla, a woman with a colorful history. His wife, Doña Felipa Perestrello e Moniz, had died not long after their son, Diego, was born. Columbus did not remarry, although in 1486 he took up with a young peasant orphan, Beatriz Enríquez de Harana, who gave birth to their son, Ferdinand. Although Columbus almost certainly never married Beatriz Enríquez—an arrangement not uncommon at the time, and perhaps never lived with her after the initial voyage—he was otherwise solicitous of Beatriz until his death. In a codicil to his will, he charged their son, Diego, to see that she was able "to live honorably, as a person to whom I am in so great debt, and thus for discharge of my conscience, because it weigheth much on my mind." These things we know, but of dalliance in the isles with Governor Beatriz we have little more than whatever inclination toward romance readers might possess.

His journal also makes no reference to a local situation of far greater import. When Columbus arrived, the Canaries had not yet been entirely subjugated by Spain. Through cruelty and treachery on several of the islands, the Spanish were forcing the native Guanches into slavery and Christianity, a practice soon to be repeated across the ocean on a continental scale. During the very summer the Captain General was there, the Guanches still held their own on the volcano island of Tenerife, but the conquest of La Palma was under way. Nothing in the logbook alludes to these struggles. Since part of the Columbian mission was to bring the subjects of the Grand Khan in Asia under the dominion of Spanish religion, it's fair to wonder whether Columbus saw any foreshadowings in the struggles of the Guanches.

With *Pinta* repaired, *Niña* rerigged, and all three ships reprovisioned, the stores stacked to the gunwales, the fleet on the sixth of September drew up its anchors in the Old World for the last time. What bottom they would touch next, Columbus had no certain idea, but he was confident it was not far distant, for he believed in the notions of several ancient authorities who held that the Atlantic was narrow; in the Canaries he recorded that many "honorable Spaniards" there swore that each year they saw land to the west. Could that place they thought they saw be Saint Brendan's Isle, a phantom then appearing on ocean charts and continuing to until the eighteenth century? Could it be Antillia, another phantom that would eventually give its name to the West Indies? Was it one of the outlier islands many geographers then believed to lie off the coast of Cathay (China)? Principal among those islands was Cipango (Japan), and it was directly for there that Columbus headed on the next leg of the voyage.

three

That none of the crew deserted during their twenty-five days in the Canary Islands suggests that the men were not beset by ancient fears about the Ocean Sea. They did not believe they were going to sail off the edge of the world and tumble willy-nilly into space. Everybody but the most benighted of that time knew the world was a sphere, and certainly sailors knew that above all others: How else to explain why a seaman atop a mast can see farther than he can from the deck or why he espies the masts of an approaching ship before the hull comes into view? Some of the men might have had notions about sea monsters, and it's likely all believed great and dangerous shoals could lie before them. Columbus himself considered it possible the fleet might come upon lands inhabited by humans with heads in the middle of their chests, or people with tails, or men with the faces of dogs. Of all the fears, the greatest among the crew and the ones Columbus had to work against almost daily after the ships were well into uncharted water was the belief they would sail too far from Europe to be able to return home against contrary winds.

He surely instructed the sailors in his belief that the distance from the Canaries to Cipango was only 2,400 nautical miles, and—fortunately for them—the islands lay at virtually the same latitude (as in fact they nearly do); all the ships had to do was hold a course directly west. If the fleet were to come upon unknown islands on the way to Asia, they would be useful to reprovision before bringing in rewards of discovery.

His years of studying both ancient and contemporary geographers and travelers (including Marco Polo who wrote his account while incarcerated in, of all places, Genoa) convinced Columbus that Asia was a land stretching so far north and south that no westering sailor could miss it if his nerve and will did not fail him; nor, so he believed, was distance really much of a concern since the Atlantic was narrower than most learned men of his time assumed. In the years prior to departing, when Columbus was trying to convince various royal scientific committees about the feasibility of his voyage, the major disagreement wasn't, as is popularly supposed, whether the world was flat, but rather how wide the Ocean Sea was. Many of the scholars opposing Columbus were closer to the truth than he, but as a man of medieval mind, he worked at things deductively: he knew where he wanted to go both in logic and on the sea, and he searched out views to support his own. We shall see this propensity again. The many, many annotations in three of his books of cosmology and geography reveal his geographical conceptions and his absolute stubbornness against admitting any evidence that might overturn his deep urge to find a westward sea route to the riches of the Indies. In his copy of Pierre d'Ailly's *Imago Mundi (Image of the World)*, Columbus noted sentences like this: "Between the end of Spain and the beginning of India is no great width," and "Water runs from pole to pole between the end of Spain and the beginning of India," and "This [Ocean] Sea is navigable in a few days with a fair wind."

Nevertheless, knowing his men's fear of sailing past a point of return that would doom them, Columbus cautiously, wisely, kept two figures for the distance the ships covered each day: one he believed accurate and the other a deliberate underestimation to report to the crew. The lower figure also served to keep expectations down and increase their tolerance of long days with no signs of landfall. Some of them surely had heard that to reach Asia by a westerly sea route would require a fleet capable of being outfitted for a three-year round trip; and since it seemed unlikely there could be any undiscovered lands between Europe and Asia for reprovisioning vessels, the crew believed men on such a voyage would perish at sea. As a discoverer, Columbus was a lucky man—even the geographical errors he made often worked to advance his goal. His achievements were the result of many things: incredible determination, fearlessness, capital abilities as a navigator and leader. But none was more important than his capacity to persuade Ferdinand and Isabella, especially the Queen, of the possibility of his correct notions. Had the American continents not been in the way, his sailors likely would have died before reaching Japan, a land almost five times farther from Spain than he calculated.

Of all the notations in his various books, one from Seneca, the Spanish-Roman philosopher and playwright, is most revealing: "An age will come after many years when the Ocean will loose the chains of things, and a huge land lie revealed; when Tiphys will disclose new worlds and Thule [Iceland] no more be the ultimate." Again, an error encouraged Columbus: Tiphys is the *pilot* of Jason's ship of legend, *Argo;* but the name Seneca actually wrote was Tethys, a sea nymph. The irony is that the Columbian version of the prophecy, whether mis-copied or not, more accurately describes what he truly found than what he meant to find.

four

Out of the Canaries, Columbus met with winds light and variable enough to keep the fleet from making significant progress until the early morning of the second day when a northeast breeze came on to move the ships westward. He had heard in the islands that Portuguese caravels were lurking nearby with a plan of either capturing his vessels or merely warning him to stay out of certain waters controlled by Portugal. Wherever those ships were, Columbus never encountered them, and his early difficulties came not from a rival nation but from *Santa María* herself plunging heavily and taking water over the bow so severely that she kept the fleet from making more than about one mile an hour. With heavy provisions restowed, the flagship leveled out and regained her speed to allow the flotilla to cover 130 miles by the following morning; on the fourth evening, the high volcano at Tenerife had slipped into invisibility. Now before the ships lay only ocean uncharted except in the imaginations of a few cartographers. Columbus must have felt the sea, its threat and promise, as never before, and surely his greatest aspiration, the Enterprise of the Indies, at last seemed eminently achievable.

The route he chose would allow him, so he reasoned, a chance to discover the long-presumed island of Antillia where the fleet might reprovision and, further, could claim such a crucial jumping-off place for the Spanish Crown and thereby return the first dividend. Even though Columbus selected what he thought the shortest and simplest route to reach Asia, a decision based upon his textual research and upon his previous experiences in the eastern Atlantic, he couldn't have known how far the prevailing winds and currents of that latitude would aid him. His course, incidentally, is very close to one used today by sailing ships going from Europe to the West Indies. Had he departed from the Azores, islands due west of the Iberian peninsula but north of his route, he would have been fighting contrary winds and soon, in all likelihood, a mutinous crew. By leaving from the Canaries, a place the ancients called the Fortunate Islands, Columbus manifested the kind of shrewdness that makes luck almost a concomitant. Were two massive continents with the longest cordillera on the planet not blocking his path, his course indeed would have taken him close to southern Japan; as it was, he was heading for the Virgin Islands.

Soon after escaping the Canary calms, a crewman spotted the broken mast of a ship, a floating timber that could be useful in repairs or as firewood, but the men were unable to take it aboard. Whether that flotsam gave any of the mariners pause about the unknown sea they were entering, an ocean that could break up stout vessels, Columbus doesn't say.

A somewhat commonplace perception now exists that the three Columbian vessels were mere cockleshells. It's true that even the flagship *Santa María,* the largest of them, was not big for that time, but she and the other two were more than adequate for an Atlantic crossing. Each was well built, and once *Niña* was refitted, they all performed capably on an open sea and—the flagship excepted—were useful for explorations along shorelines.

Although no pictures of any kind depicting the vessels survive, we have some idea of their appearance from comments in the logbook and from comparison with other similar ships of the era. The several replicas of this famous trio constructed over the last century all derive from informed guesswork in shape, size, and rigging. *Santa María* was a *não*—"ship" in Portuguese—commonly used to transport cargo, and she was slower and less maneuverable than her consorts, which were of a type called caravels; never was *María* the favorite of Columbus, despite her more commodious captain's quarters. Her three masts carried white sails decorated with crosses and heraldic symbols. In all probability, *María* was less than eighty feet long, her beam or width less than thirty, her draft when loaded about seven feet. As with the others, her sides above the waterline were painted in bright colors, and below the line dark pitch covered the hull to discourage shipworms and barnacles.

All the vessels were closed to the sea—these were not the open boats of Leif Eriksson—and each presumably had a raised section aft, the poop deck where stood the officer of the watch and often Columbus. Beneath it was the helmsman; unable to see ahead, this steersman worked the heavy tiller connected to the large outboard rudder according to a compass, commands from the poop deck, and the feel of the ship herself in wind and water. Below the main deck were sets of oars used to create steerageway in calms or to maneuver in shallows or move in or out of port. In the lowest area of the vessel were bilge pumps to empty seawater that finds its way into nearly any boat.

The crew, about forty men on the flagship and somewhat fewer on *Pinta* and *Niña,* slept wherever they could find an open and reasonably level space on deck or atop something; during clement nights, they slept topside but had to crowd below in hard weather or rough seas. After noticing on the First Voyage the hammocks of the Indians, sailors began creating for themselves more pleasant shipboard sleep. The officers in their quarters had actual small berths. Heads, or "latrines," were nothing more than several seats hanging over the rails both fore and aft, an arrangement that often provided an unexpected and probably not entirely unwelcome washing.

Each ship had a firebox for cooking; carried either on deck or in fair weather towed behind to free up deck space was a longboat or launch used to reach a wharf or beach or to sound shallows. Armaments were light and for defense or signaling only; individual arms consisted of crossbows, clumsy muskets, and the ubiquitous sailor's knife. The expedition was one of exploration and not military conquest because Columbus assumed the Grand Khan and other leaders in Asia would willingly place themselves under the authority of Spain, then more a loose collection of small kingdoms than one nation we know today.

Second in size was *Pinta,* the ship we know least about. Like *Niña,* she was a caravel, staunch craft that operated nicely in windward work yet were still nimble enough to allow sailing in shallow water. *Pinta* made several later Atlantic crossings, her last one in 1500 when a hurricane overtook and capsized her in the southern Bahamas less than two hundred miles from where *Santa María* left her bones.

For sailing qualities, Columbus favored *Niña,* the ship he would return home in after *María* came to grief; he included *Niña* on both his Second and Third Voyages to the New World. Although the smallest of the three, she had four masts; the eminent naval historian and blue-water sailor Samuel Eliot Morison said *Niña* was "one of the greatest little ships in the world's history," yet she disappeared just seven years after her first voyage to America.

Spanish ships of that era carried both a religious name and a nickname. *Santa María* was known to her sailors as *La Gallega,* perhaps because she was built in Galicia; *Niña,* formally the *Santa Clara,* took her popular name from her owner, Juan Niño. For *Pinta,* neither her religious name nor how she came by her sobriquet has come down to us. In the annals of seafaring, nowhere else are the names of three otherwise ordinary ships so widely known.

five

Because of a potentially restive crew, one not accustomed to being out of sight of land for days on end, Columbus had considerable concern about the resolution of his men to reach Asia, and he seized upon whatever he could to keep them believing the great eastern continent lay not far distant. Initially, pelagic birds served this end well. On the fourteenth of September, sailors on *Niña* reported seeing a tern and a tropic bird, species Columbus incorrectly—or conveniently—insisted kept within twenty-five leagues, a moderate day's sail, of shore. For the next three and a half weeks, he recorded more than a dozen sightings of birds, events he used to stoke his crew's resolve and remind everyone to remain alert for the first view of a coast. The man who spied it would receive a reward of a coat and ten months' wages paid in an annuity underwritten by a tax on meat shops. In that way, butchers helped Columbus reach the New World. Considering the carnage of the European conquest of the Americas, this link has a certain aptness.

The logbook rarely gives any direct statements about how Columbus *felt*—what his emotions were—during the long days on an uncharted ocean; if he set down such thoughts, only a few appear in the abstract. Perhaps there once were more sentences from him like this one of the sixteenth of September: "The savor of the mornings was a great delight, for nothing was lacking except to hear nightingales." How welcome would be other similar expressions from the man who led the most significant voyage in history. How fine it would be to see the man of flesh and hopes and frailties show through! But Columbus then was not much given to musing, and he, an Italian, expresses himself in an unsophisticated Spanish.

He was seemingly incapable of self-doubt about conceptions of his God, the size of the Earth, the positions of oceans, and, later, his colossal role in the annals of discovery; yet, on that First Voyage especially, there must have been flickerings that he might have mistaken something in his geographical knowledge or misinterpreted an ancient text or misjudged the capacity of ordinary seamen to withstand trepidation natural to an expedition into unknown waters. Clearly it was to the advantage of his Enterprise for him never to admit any impediment except obvious and inescapable ones, but the consequence of such behavior is that today we see far more a commander than a man.

On that same September afternoon, the ships encountered the first bunches of gulf weed or sargassum, a floating plant that can extend for several miles, the stuff giving the Sargasso Sea its name. The vegetation did not hinder the ships; in fact, the crew, believing their leader who errantly said it was torn from a rocky shore, took heart in its appearance, ever more so when they found in it a small crab Columbus kept. The timely appearance of these living things fortuitously helped steady the men on that day when the pilots first observed their compass bearing no longer matching the position of Polaris, a circumstance the Captain General explained by telling them it was the North Star that shifted, not the needle; in this, he was mostly correct, for in 1492 Polaris prescribed a circle of more than three degrees around the boreal pole; today it varies less than a full degree. Also at work was compass variation, a phenomenon not then understood. Surely Columbus must have spent much time just before and during the crossing in educating the sailors into his geographic conceptions, since the most likely initial cause of a mutiny to force a return to Spain would be ignorance.

The next day, Martín Alonso Pinzón, captain of the swift *Pinta,* saw a large flock of birds flying westward. Believing they were moving toward shore, he let his caravel run ahead of her companions in hope of spotting land first and claiming the sizable and remunerative honor. Columbus well realized that one of the comforting sights for the sailors was to look across the blank face of the ocean and catch sight of two other Spanish ships, just as he also knew fragmentation of the fleet not only would have grave consequences for their survival, but Pinzón's independent action could set a precedent that might foster a demand to turn back for Spain. Such a homeward retreat, however, was not likely to come from Pinzón himself, whose eagerness to discover unknown islands or establish the location of long-presumed ones matched Columbus's determination to find a western route to the Indies. *Pinta* returned the following day, but it was not the last time her capricious captain would break ranks in pursuit of his own ends.

The appearance that afternoon of a massive bank of

clouds to the north reinforced the Captain General's conviction that the fleet was indeed near land, but his overriding objective, unlike Pinzón's, was to reach Cipango, the great island off the coast of Asia that would serve as a stepping-stone to arrival in the Indies. Rather than chasing chimeric places, Columbus held course due west and presumed the return voyage would serve to discover long-supposed Atlantic isles. In this way, he proved himself a wiser navigator and a more reliable leader than the avaricious Pinzón.

Those who have argued, often for nationalistic reasons, that Martín Pinzón was the true commander of the Enterprise of the Indies and that Columbus was only titular head must reckon among other things with the Spaniard's impulsiveness. Could such a man, undoubtedly an able mariner, ever have succeeded in the endeavor? Of the nearly hundred sailors afloat that day far out on a strange ocean that could turn lethal in moments, there was but *one* man who had the geographical knowledge, navigational skill, unyielding determination, and shrewd leadership to reach the far side of the Atlantic. It was not Martín Alonso Pinzón.

six

The next several days provided more incidents from nature that assisted Columbus in holding the crew steady in *his* resolve: the continuation of sargassum was some reassurance, but even more significant was a pair of birds that fluttered aboard *Santa María* and began singing. A seaman caught another bird which, upon examination, the Captain General averred (again incorrectly) to be a river species. On that evening he writes: "A booby came from the west-northwest and went southeast, which was a sign that it left land to the west-northwest, because these birds sleep on land and in the morning go out to sea to hunt for food and do not go farther than 20 leagues from land." The next day a whale surfaced, another supposed indication of a shore somewhere near.

But to Columbus the most helpful of the natural occurrences was the wind shifting against them to blow across the bows and into their faces. He says, "This contrary wind was of much use to me, because my people were all worked up thinking that no winds blew in these waters for returning to Spain." But a situation the following afternoon created potential for more fretting by the men when a calm sea quickly turned rough without apparent cause, a condition astounding everyone. The Captain General, missing no chance to urge on his crew, played this change into a biblical allusion with grand implications to support his crafty leadership; he writes: "Very useful to me was the high sea, [a sign] such as had not appeared save in the time of the Jews when they came up out of Egypt [and grumbled] against Moses who delivered them out of captivity."

On September twenty-fifth, Columbus and Pinzón

had a conversation—the ships alongside in the calm water—with both men agreeing there must be islands nearby. But where were they? Soon after, while the Commander was trying to replot their position, Pinzón suddenly appeared on the poop deck of *Pinta* and in much excitement called over the quiet sea that he was claiming the reward for spotting land. Columbus rushed out, dropped to his knees in thanks, and each ship resounded with *Gloria in excelsis Deo.* Sailors went up the masts and riggings on *Niña,* and until dark, everybody on every vessel stared at the shadowy shore. The fleet altered course from west to southwest toward it. In the slick water, the men celebrated with a swim and a salty bath, their joy enhanced by creatures long a delight to anyone at sea, porpoises.

By morning the ebullience was gone. The "land" had been nothing more than clouds on the horizon, a condition that often fools seafarers, sometimes disastrously. Again the fleet turned westward. For such a phantom not to have appeared at all would have been better than for the sailors to undergo an abrupt deflation of a sweet expectation. It may be telling of their temperament during the next few days that they killed several porpoises.

As the miles through calm water continued, doubts about the ships being able to sail home before depleting their fresh water must have rekindled. In retrospect, we can see today that had the fleet faced continuous and reassuring, homeward-bound winds, it's unlikely the expedition could have held out long enough against them to reach the western side of the Atlantic. Columbus faced a quandary: Whatever direction the wind blew or didn't blow, there was peril.

The large number of birds in several flocks and the variety of species convinced him the birds were not simply strays or wanderers, and this time he was correct, for the great autumnal migrations had begun. Watching the flights pass so easily and swiftly, the mariners must have envied them as wings overtook the ships slogging along in near calms. Even the flying fish moved faster. By the first of October, doubts and discontents, and irritations of confined and uncertain men increased to a dangerous degree. No one aboard any of the vessels had ever been so long out of sight of land. Columbus finally concluded the flotilla had somehow passed through the string of islands he believed lay east of Cipango, evidence that should have alerted him to the difference between his imaginatively filled-in chart and the truth of the Atlantic, yet he apparently used the absence of the presumed isles as further proof that he was beyond Cipango and nearing Cathay. His deductive mind was not to change easily, if at all, but, as with so many other aspects of his career at sea, even this error benefited him, even if in no way other than protecting him from potential doubts.

On the morning of October seventh, swift *Niña,* having pulled ahead of the fleet to give those men the best chance of claiming the reward, raised a flag on her tallest mast and fired a small cannon to signal that her crew had spotted land. *Pinta* and *Santa María* soon came up and for the rest of the day their crewmen strained to see what the *Niña* sailors had claimed, but before them was only more ocean. After that, Columbus declared that another false *"Tierra!"* would disqualify a man from the reward.

Earlier, he had ordered the ships to gather close to him each sunrise and sunset, ostensibly to equalize the competition for a initial sighting at the time when light is most favorable for seeing far, but he was also aware that his slow flagship gained an advantage with its high mast. The great Enterprise was his idea, and he wanted to be the man history would record as the first to sight some far piece of Asia after a westward voyage.

Observing the numbers of birds passing to the southwest reminded him that the Portuguese had discovered the farthest Azores by following avian flocks—and perhaps also considering Pinzón's urge to change course to a more southwesterly one—Columbus decided to deviate for two days from his due westward heading to take up a rhumb aligned with the flights of terns and boobies, a decision that would change history. Even in the darkness the sailors heard the migrating birds: If there were sounds or sights that could give them reassurance short of a breaking surf or a tree-girt isle, those aerial flappings and squawkings, the winged silhouettes against a bright moon, must have served.

25

Despite his phony reckonings, everyone knew by then the ships were well beyond the area Columbus had predicted they would find land. He was increasingly alone in his insistence on continuing west, and it didn't help that of all the men, he was one of only five who were not Spaniards. His very accent must have isolated him yet further.

Columbus did what a good commander should do. He held counsel with the three captains, listened, and compromised enough to gain their further temporary acceptance of his plan: If after three days the expedition had come upon no land, he would then, and only then, turn homeward. Or so he said.

Various legal depositions made many years later by pro-Pinzón sailors claimed it was Columbus who wanted to give up and Martín Alonso who demanded the flotilla continue west, but their evidence is too biased, too much challenged by other witnesses and events, and, above all, too far out of keeping with the character of Columbus to be credible. A person driven by both an idea and an ideal, one who believes his God favors his work, will outlast those motivated only by money. Columbus was in no way averse to financial compensation for his long efforts, but that was not the primary goal then pushing him. For him, his compelling geographical concept, one in his mind underwritten by a deity, was the force that would drive the three ships on toward opening new riches to Europe.

On the tenth of October the fleet made its longest twenty-four-hour run of the entire outbound voyage, nearly two hundred miles, but by that point leagues away from home were to the crewmen more worrisome than gladsome. Of that day Las Casas says: "Here the men could no longer stand it; they complained of the long voyage. But [Columbus] encouraged them as best he could, giving them good hope of the benefits that they would be able to secure. And he added that it was useless to complain since he had come to find the Indies and thus had to continue the voyage until he found them, with the help of Our Lord."

Despite this wise combination of encouragement and adamantine will, how easy could the Captain General's sleep have been then? What was to prevent mutinous sailors from pitching him overboard—reported as an accident—and then turning the ships toward home? Perhaps it was their commander's force of character, or the influence of the three ship captains, or maybe it was their belief that he was the man most capable of getting them safely returned. Whatever held Columbus in precarious security during those days of increasing tension and unrest, he knew the men's resolution and forbearance of mutiny would not likely last much longer. When the threads holding the enterprise together were ready to snap, he was only hours away from setting down the most momentous entry ever in any nautical record.

seven

On Thursday, the eleventh of October, a strong trade wind kicked up the roughest sea the ships had yet encountered, but new kinds of flotsam cheered them: freshly green reeds and cane, a branch full of blossoms, a small plank, and, above all, a "little stick fashioned with iron." Columbus, now certain that a landfall was just ahead, addressed the sailors of *María* to urge them to greater vigilance and remind them of the reward waiting the mariner with the keenest eyes.

At sundown he brought his course back to due west, a change that may have prevented a reefing, and he rescinded his recent order to do no night sailing, surely to give himself a greater chance to cover more miles before the three days were up. To move so swiftly in dark, unknown waters added to an atmosphere already tense with expectation and competition. He who called out a false sighting would lose the reward, and he who waited a moment too long could lose his life. Martín Pinzón in *Pinta* led the way.

At ten that evening, the moon, a little past full, was yet an hour from rising when Columbus thought he saw a firelight, a *lumbre,* but he was so uncertain he asked a servant—not an officer—to confirm it; that fellow also thought he could see it from moment to moment. But a third underling detected nothing. The light, writes Columbus, "was like a little wax candle lifting and rising."

Then an able seaman, Pedro Yzquierdo, cried out, "*Lumbre! Tierra!*" Columbus calmly responded, "I saw and spoke of that light, which is on land, some time ago." Then it vanished for everybody. Was there actually a light? With the fleet at least thirty-five miles from land, it's more plausible the *lumbre* was a natural conjuration not uncommon on a dark ocean, especially to watchers straining to see something specific. The next day Columbus must have realized as much, yet he would use that ephemeral and uncertified luminescence to claim the reward for himself. His motive was less likely greed than the natural unwillingness of a man who gives most of his life to an idea only to have an uninformed latecomer pop up to claim it. For Columbus, the light could be the first real proof of his vigorous contention about the narrow width of the Ocean Sea; for him, *that* was the greater prize; in fact, he did not keep the annuity but gave it to Beatriz Enríquez, the mother of his younger son. As for Pedro Yzquierdo, he was so angered at losing the reward he later renounced Christianity to become a Muslim.

The night wore on, the spectral sails full under the moon, prows slicing through the black swells, sailors tiring and reluctantly giving in to sleep. Those who dozed off were to wake in not just the New World of the Americas but into a new world of concepts and commodities, politics and possibilities, genes and genocides. Even the one man on board whose comprehension and imagination extended furthest, he the commander, soon to be

Admiral of the Ocean Sea, would never quite understand what those wooden prows were cutting open.

eight

On Friday, October twelfth, at two in the morning, Juan Rodríguez Bermejo aboard *Pinta* sang out to his shipmates, "*Tierra! Tierra!*" Ahead, illuminated dimly by moonlight lay a whitish bluff above a dark shoreline. To Columbus it had to be some part of Asia, perhaps one of the islands off Japan. He and a few others were right after all! Hadn't he proved the distance from Europe to the Far East was not great? His flotilla had crossed the Ocean Sea in only thirty-three days on a voyage not especially difficult. (The 1607 English voyage to establish Jamestown, Virginia, took four and half months.) Except for the uncertainty of the crewmen, the ease of it was far more remarkable than all of its difficulties combined.

This much is correct: He had turned two millennia of geographic theorizing about the Atlantic—most of it incorrect, some fantastically so—into arcane lore fit only for texts about ancient history. In just over a month, three small wooden ships with hulls shaped like pecans had remade the map of the blue planet. Wealth beyond anyone's dreams now surely lay before the mariners. But had Columbus known where he truly was, he would have been deeply disappointed. He wasn't much interested in finding a paired continental mass the size of Asia, because he wanted to pioneer a new sea route to the ready riches of the Orient, and he wanted the wealth and recognition that would go with that. Beyond those ends, he desired for Christendom the souls of all the inhabitants of lands new to Europe.

Martín Alonso Pinzón, verifying the sighting, ordered a cannon fired to signal the other ships as his men took in sail so *Niña* and *María* could catch up; when they did, Columbus called across the water, "Martín Alonso! You have found land!" Pinzón answered, "Sir, my reward is not lost!" Columbus, apparently already having decided to keep the annuity—and coat—as recompense for his spotting the mysterious light, offered consolation that must have been anything but satisfying: "I give you five thousand maravedís as a present!" Seaman Bermejo (also known as Rodrigo de Triana), the actual first European to lay eyes on a shore of the New World since the Northmen five centuries earlier, apparently received nothing.

Precisely where was this shore, this small island called Guanahani by its residents and soon to be renamed San Salvador by Columbus? Everyone agrees it was either in the Bahaman archipelago or in the Caicos, the southern extension of the Bahamas, all told more than seven hundred islands, islets, and cays. Over the past century and a half, scholars and mariners have proposed nine different places, several too far-fetched to be credible. The most reliable historians cite one of two islands, only sixty miles apart: Watling or Samana Cay. The British in 1926 changed Watling to San Salvador as if to end speculation, but recent evidence creates a strong case for Samana Cay.

The Spanish ships made short tacks back and forth near the coast until daylight could reveal a safe anchorage from which the longboats could take some of the men, all armed, to shore. As dawn began to unveil the island, the Europeans could see just past a narrow strand of white beach, a low and rather level place, intensely green beyond the bright sand. The sun rising behind them spread golden light across groves of tropical hardwoods, and almost immediately, naked people painted red, white, and black in a variety of patterns emerged from the trees to stare at what surely was the strangest thing ever to appear before them. Their curiosity was greater than their concern, and they stood expectantly.

Able seamen oared the launches carrying Columbus, the three captains, officers, and officials, including an interpreter versed in Arabic and Hebrew—widely considered ancestral to all languages—through the foreshore and onto the sand. Amidst the surf and the flap and flourish of flags and banners, someone made that first momentary and momentous footfall. Given his character and sense of destiny, it seems likely it was Columbus himself. He knelt and "with tears of joy" gave thanks to his God, then arose and named the island San Salvador—Holy Savior—and summoned all his men to bear witness to his taking possession of the land in the name of his Sovereigns and according to papal decrees. Had the natives understood the language or the import of the proceedings, we can imagine their incredulity at some stranger merely stepping onto a beach and saying, in effect, "What was yours is now ours."

The Spaniards hailed Columbus, his son Ferdinand would write, as Admiral and Viceroy with joy and victory, "all begging his pardon for the injuries that through fear and inconstancy they had done him." Even knowing the rueful history that Europeans were about to inflict on the Americas, one can envision the triumph, fulfillment, self-justification, and relief flooding him.

After that great footfall, the character of Columbus revealed itself in new ways. At that point, Las Casas quotes directly an utterance of prime importance to the history of the Western Hemisphere; with these words one can say Euro-American history begins:

I, in order that they would be friendly to us—because I recognized that they were people who would be better freed [from error] and converted to our Holy Faith by love than by force—to some of them I gave red caps, and glass beads they put on their chests, and many other things of small value, in which they took so much pleasure and became so much our friends that it was a marvel. Later they came swimming to the ships' launches where we

were and brought us parrots and cotton thread in
balls and javelins and many other things, and they
traded them to us for other things we gave them,
such as small glass beads and [hawk] bells. In sum,
they took everything and gave of what they had
very willingly. But it seemed to me that they were a
people very poor in everything. All of them go
around as naked as their mothers bore them; and
the women also, although I did not see more than
one quite young girl. And all those that I saw were
young people, for none did I see of more than 30
years of age. They are very well formed, with handsome bodies and good faces. Their hair [is] coarse—
almost like the tail of a horse—and short. They wear
their hair down over their eyebrows except for a little in the back which they wear long and never cut.
Some of them paint themselves with black, and they
are of the color of the Canarians, neither black nor
white; and some of them paint themselves with
white, and some of them with red, and some of
them with whatever they find. And some of them
paint their faces, and some of them the whole body,
and some of them only the eyes, and some of them
only the nose. They do not carry arms nor are they
acquainted with them, because I showed them
swords and they took them by the edge and
through ignorance cut themselves. They have no
iron. Their javelins are shafts without iron and

some of them have at the end a fish tooth and others of other things. All of them alike are of good-sized stature and carry themselves well. I saw some who had marks of wounds on their bodies and I made signs to them asking what they were; and they showed me how people from other islands nearby came there and tried to take them, and how they defended themselves; and I believed and believe that they come here from *tierra firme* [Asia] to take them captive. They should be good and intelligent servants, for I see that they say very quickly everything that is said to them; and I believe that they would become Christians very easily, for it seemed to me that they had no religion. Our Lord pleasing, at the time of my departure I will take six of them from here to Your Highnesses in order that they may learn to speak. No animal of any kind did I see on this island except parrots.

These aboriginals, the Lucayo tribe, were of the Taino culture, spoke a dialect of the Arawak language, and descended from people living along the coast of northwest South America. They cultivated corn, tubers, casava, and peppers; they fished and caught crabs; they spun and wove cotton, made decorated pottery, and fashioned ornaments of shell and bone. Their frame houses had palm-thatch roofs, and they were expert in moving large dugout canoes over the open sea. Some of these craft were longer than a Spanish caravel. Perhaps most curious was their practice of head-binding infants to produce high and flat foreheads, a mark of beauty and distinction to them. Although Columbus could not or refused to discern it, the Tainos lived by spiritual concepts and practices. Most significantly, once they understood the Spanish plans, they were not willing to become servants and certainly not slaves.

Of all the inferences in Columbus's long and often complimentary description of them—one of the warmest ever made by an invader—none is of darker import than his initial hint of slavery made immediately after the first encounter with the Tainos. This primal statement about the eventual European conquest of the Americas contains seeds that five hundred years later still poison descendants from both hemispheres.

nine

How an encounter of such magnitude could begin so cordially only to turn so quickly into extermination is not difficult to explain. Samuel Eliot Morison says it clearly: "[The] guilelessness and generosity of the simple savage aroused the worst traits of cupidity and brutality in the average European. Even the Admiral's humanity seems to have been merely political, as a means to eventual enslavement and exploitation." A modern reader following his life up to his arrival in the Bahamas sees a man one can readily admire: intelligent, dedicated, persuasive, a capable leader. But on that fateful October Friday in 1492, Columbus demonstrated behavior deserving the adjective "reprehensible."

On Saturday morning, some Spaniards went ashore to engage in the standard activities of sailors on liberty—sightseeing, trading for souvenirs, and, surely, a few undertakings of the flesh—while numerous Lucayos paddled dugout canoes up to the ships. In his journal entry for that day, Columbus reiterates in fair detail his flattering view of the natives as "handsome in body." The shipboard crewmen traded various trinkets as well as pieces of broken crockery and glass, even torn pieces of clothing. Columbus says of the Lucayos, "They brought balls of spun cotton and parrots and javelins and other little things that it would be tiresome to write down, and they gave everything for anything that was given to them. I was attentive and labored to find out if there was any gold." With that last sentence and that single word "gold," the second leg of the conquest steps forward and is ready to march.

On Sunday, in the longboats, Columbus and several officers and men rowed to the other side of Guanahani where they met a second enthusiastic welcome. Lucayos hailed them, jumped into the water and swam to the Spaniards, and one old man, perhaps a spiritual leader, climbed into a boat and shouted to his people, "Come and see the men who came from the sky! Bring them food and drink!" Columbus does not say how he could possibly have understood the Lucayo words, but we can be certain the interpreter of Hebrew and Arabic was utterly useless. Clearly, the Captain General's recording that the natives mistook the Europeans for heavenly creatures served his own goals, and for that reason we should be suspicious of it.

The generous and peaceable acts of bringing food and water out to the sailors Columbus interprets as another indication of their potential for servility. He writes:

> These people are very naive about weapons, as Your Highnesses will see from seven that I caused to be taken in order to carry them away to you and to learn our language and to return them. Except that, whenever Your Highnesses may command, all of them can be taken to Castile or held captive in this same island; because with 50 men all of them could be held in subjection and can be made to do whatever one might wish.

We can visualize Columbus in his quarters aboard *Santa María* that evening, dipping into his ink and setting down the events of the first forty-eight hours of Spain in the Americas, two days that were wonderful for everyone of both races and cultures, each side reflecting on the events with a different kind of innocence and naiveté. Many Americans' comprehension of that first great encounter ends right there; they have not followed the history beyond those initial idyllic moments, a short view that leads to a chauvinism evident even in the eminent historian Samuel Eliot Morison: "Never again may mortal men hope to recapture the amazement, the wonder, the delight of those October days in 1492 when the New World gracefully yielded her virginity to the conquering Castilians."

ten

Columbus departed Guanahani at dawn on the fifteenth of October in search of gold, a commodity that could make his expedition profitably successful in the eyes of Ferdinand and Isabella, as well as virtually proving—so he reasoned—that the islands were near those his charts showed lying not far east of the gold-rich Asian coast. Further, he had his own expeditionary debts to pay off. For the remainder of the First Voyage, this particular quest overwhelmed his search for Cipango and Cathay, although he was staking royal claims to lands and peoples as he went. "It was my wish," he says, "to bypass no island without taking possession, although having taken one you can claim all."

Of several Lucayos forcibly hauled aboard to serve as guides and eventually interpreters, one escaped in the night, and another leaped into the sea and got away in a dugout with men from a farther island who approached the fleet. Probably concerned about what the Lucayos might say to their kinsmen, Columbus sent sailors ashore in pursuit, but the natives "fled like chickens" into the woods. Soon after, when a lone man paddled up to trade a ball of cotton, Spaniards jumped into the water and dragged him aboard *Niña*. Watching it all from the poop deck of *Santa María*, Columbus sent for him in order to give him baubles used successfully in the West African trade; the seamen set upon his head a bright red cap and wound around his arm green glass beads and hung two hawk bells (used by falconers) on his ears before returning his canoe and releasing him. These acts were not humanitarian gestures, but rather practical strategy, as the Captain General reveals when the fleet came upon a second native carrying in his dugout a fist-size piece of bread, a calabash of water, and a little powdered red earth—probably for body paint—and "some dry leaves, which must be something highly esteemed among them." Columbus writes:

> Later I saw on land [the man] to whom I had given the things aforesaid and whose ball of cotton I had not wanted to take from him, although he wanted to give it to me—[and I saw] that all the others went up to him. He considered it a great marvel, and indeed it seemed to him that we were good people and that the other man who had fled had done us some harm and that for this we were taking

him with us. And the reason that I behaved in this way toward him, ordering him set free and giving him the things mentioned, was in order that they would hold us in their esteem so that, when Your Highnesses some other time again send people here, the natives will receive them well. And everything that I gave him was not worth four maravedís.

A *maravedí* was a coin of small value. Columbus was right. When the first slavers not long after reached that area of the Caribbean, they found the natives hospitable, trusting, and hardly suspecting capture.

He expresses the meaning of his phrase "receive them well" more bluntly in describing his treatment of another lone trader: "[I returned] his belongings in order that, through good reports of us—our Lord pleasing—when Your Highnesses send [others] here, those who come will receive courteous treatment and the natives will give us all that they may have." And were those esteemed leaves tobacco?

The logbook contains numerous instances of Lucayan warmth and generosity tendered to the Christians, the term both Las Casas and Ferdinand often use in referring to the Europeans. Columbus describes one incident that is representative of several others: "I sent the ship's boat to shore for water. And the natives very willingly showed my people where the water was, and they themselves brought the filled barrels to the boat and delighted in pleasing us."

In coursing through the Bahamas under the pilotage of the captured Lucayos as well as accepting direction from others on shore, Columbus was intent on finding an island or city called Samoet reportedly rich with gold, the kind of quest that would continue later on both American continents as Spaniards followed instructions of the aboriginal inhabitants toward an El Dorado or Quivira. Hard is the modern heart that cannot applaud the natives for so quickly comprehending the necessity and efficacy of sending avaricious Europeans onward to some forever-distant golden kingdom.

Several sailors exploring an island reported to Columbus they had come upon a villager wearing a large nose plug of gold shaped like a coin with some sort of markings on it, but the Lucayo refused to part with his decoration. Upon hearing about the ornament, Columbus thought its marks might be a Japanese or Chinese inscription, further evidence of his arrival in Asia. He upbraided the men for not offering enough to come away with the diagnostic ornament.

Of several things one may say favorably about this first Spanish quest for gold in the Western Hemisphere, Columbus's recording details of the peoples and natural history of the Caribbean preserved much information otherwise lost had a lesser explorer—say a Pizzaro or Ponce de León—been commander. While Columbus is no Las Casas in his reporting, nevertheless, among the conquistadors, almost none left anything other than devastation behind.

As the first expeditionary describer of the Americas, the frequent accuracy and resistance to fables in the accounts by Columbus makes his reports generally reliable. Even if Columbus, in order to prove the worth of his expedition, sometimes gives a suspiciously glowing account of the New World, his journal still proves reasonably sound except for some naïve assumptions and incorrect interpretations. The most famous of these, of course, was his fixedly unalterable geographical beliefs. On his fifth day in the Caribbean he makes the first reference to the natives as Indians (*Yndios*), therewith initiating an error that to this day vexes languages, communication, and some aboriginal Americans themselves. In the fifteenth century, people spoke of three Indias or Indies: the subcontinent we today call by that name as well as Asia and eastern Africa.

In his plain but serviceable style, Columbus describes curious flora (including corn and tobacco) and fish, plants and creatures unlike anything he'd ever before come across, but among the small islands he reports finding no "animals of any sort except lizards and parrots." About the people he says he "saw cotton cloths made like small cloaks . . . and the women wear [in] in front of their bodies a little thing of cotton that scarcely covers their genitals." He reports that the interiors of Lucayan dwellings "were well swept and clean and that their beds and furnishings were made of things like cotton nets. The houses are all made like Moorish campaign tents, very high and with good smoke holes." This is the first European encounter with hammocks, something the Spanish would soon adopt for shipboard use and that continued even into the American navy after World War II.

Despite doing much of his exploration during the rainy season, Columbus yet could say to his Sovereigns of this New World, his Indies, "Your Highnesses may believe that this land is the best and most fertile and temperate and level and goodly that there is in the world." If he gives a nearly utopian view of the islands—one that advances his ends—he still never descends into the fabulations of the pseudonymous Sir John Mandeville's purported travels to the Near East and India.

eleven

For the next several days, Columbus followed the arm and hand directions of his impressed Indian pilots. Roaming among the southeastern Bahamas, naming the larger islands (names that didn't stick), he made a few landings more to fill casks with fresh water than to investigate a place. At times he dispatched *Niña* and *Pinta* on slightly different courses to cover more area, but the Christians saw a continuation of what they'd already encountered, and descriptions in his journal often echo one another. A week after first setting foot in the Americas, Columbus goes beyond himself:

> I saw this cape to be so green and handsome, like all other things and lands of this island, so I don't know where to go first, nor can I tire my eyes from looking at such handsome verdure and so very different from ours. And I believe that there are in it many plants and many trees worth a lot in Spain for dyes and for medicines of spicery; but I don't recognize them, which gives me great grief. And, approaching this cape, there came so fair and sweet a smell of flowers or trees from the land, that it was the sweetest thing in the world.

Rare are such generous and flattering expressions among Spaniards—conquistadors or otherwise—who followed Columbus into the New World, yet passages like this are not uncommon from him, even though he knew natural beauty was neither an exportable commodity nor anything the Crown would ever care about. He could ignore the practicalities of politics and economics to speak his heart, and those utterances about the Americas reveal the noblest side of the man. If it were gold Spain wanted, who could care whether it came from a beautiful forest primeval or a denuded rock pile?

Two days later he conveys again his sense of wonder—perhaps mixed with boosterism—during that first week in a strange realm. This land, as Shakespeare would say a century later about the western Atlantic isles, was indeed a brave new world that has such creatures in it:

> Here are some great lagoons, and around them, on the banks, the verdure is marvelous; and round about there is a marvelous amount of woodland, the grass like in April in Andalusia, and the singing of the little birds such that it would seem that man would never wish to leave here; and the flocks of parrots obscured the sun, and big and little birds of all sorts, and so different from ours that it is marvelous. Furthermore—it has trees of a thousand kinds, and all have their kinds of fruit, and all so fragrant that it is marvelous; and I had the greatest chagrin in the world not to recognize them, for I am well assured that they are all things of value; and I bring specimens of them and also of the plants.

"Marvelous" four times? Those are not words of a covetous, rapacious man bent only on fame and wealth, but such outpourings, at least in the Columbian texts still extant, would decline during his later voyages.

He had his men gather bundles of what he calls aloes—probably an agave—that he mistakenly thought valuable. By this time Columbus surely understood it would have been more useful to carry along a botanist rather than an interpreter of Hebrew and Arabic. He realized how much he was missing or misinterpreting because of the language barrier, but at least one of his

Lucayo guides was beginning to pick up some Spanish words and could now serve to reassure other Indians that the white men weren't dangerous and tell his people of the curious trade goods. In his logbook, Columbus reveals an undercurrent of near frustration over not having enough time to learn the islands to discern the hidden wealth they must contain. As always, though, the lure of gold and hope for a landfall on the Asian mainland—almost one and the same thing—drew him on.

On two occasions his men killed a large iguana, a favorite native dish, and they continued to see golden nose ornaments on the Indians. Yet, searching for a chief who reportedly festooned himself in gold, Columbus says, "I don't have much faith in their speeches, as much for not understanding them well, as for being aware that they are so poor in gold that whatever little this king wears would appear a lot to them." Still thinking of long-range consequences of his actions, Columbus forbade the men entering one village—freshly emptied of fleeing Indians—to take anything, "not even of the value of a pin," a command that would soon change.

After quoting thirteen days of journal entries directly from Columbus, Las Casas again resumes his abstracting except for brief quotations, and we lose the Captain General's often evocative voice. The third-person summary statements frequently lack details, and they obscure the man himself. Except for nautical historians, the rest of us find little import in compressed sentences like, "He sailed from sunrise until 9 A.M. to the WSW; must have made about five leagues."

Believing that the Indian pilots' talk about a large island they called Colba—Cuba—must refer to Cipango, Columbus continued to follow their guidance along a route they knew from regular inter-island voyages in dugout *canoes,* a Tainoan word he introduces to European languages on his third Friday in the Caribbean. To take such craft, made from a single tree trunk, onto blue water attests to the nautical skills of the natives. Two days later, the twenty-eighth of October, Columbus reached the northeastern shore of Cuba where he found a low mountainous land even more beautiful than the small, level islands he'd been among; unlike them, it had rivers of fresh water, but where were Marco Polo's cities of alabaster with roofs tiled in gold? How could this be Japan? Columbus named the place Juana after the heir to the Spanish throne, Infante Don Juan.

During those last four days of October along what is today the Cuban coast of Oriente province, the fleet sailed from bay to bay, stopping where a good anchorage allowed the sailors to explore a few miles up a river. The Taino villages they came upon were better built and furnished than those of the Lucayos in the Bahamas—a sign to Columbus that the Asian mainland was near—but all were empty of residents who left behind everything except their clothes (given that they went about largely naked, that means they fled with virtually nothing). How different that first historic encounter on Guanahani might have been had the Lucayos been similarly fearful.

The Spaniards found barkless dogs—a source of meat, not protection, for the Indians—tamed birds (probably parrots), and "many images in the shape of women, and many heads in the shape of masks, very well worked." Whether these objects were for beauty or worship, Columbus never learned. No matter how far he explored up a river, he saw not so much as a wooden town let alone a fabulous city to match Marco Polo's old (and outdated) report, and nowhere did he come upon sailing ships of the mighty Khan for whom the Captain General carried royal letters of introduction. Yet Columbus insisted on interpreting the sign language of his Indian guides as indicating the Grand Khan lived nearby, and he understood them to say that to reach the mainland was only a voyage of ten days. Believing there were only islands between Europe and the eastern coast of Asia, to Columbus that mainland had to be Cathay! The peril in deductive reasoning is that it allows one to conclude what one wishes to conclude. By always proceeding from the general to the specific, rather than vice versa, Columbus could never know where he really was.

twelve

Contrary winds forced Columbus to return to the best Caribbean harbor he'd yet found, at what is today

Gibara, Cuba, and there the fleet remained for the next eleven days. The immense size of the island, coupled with the Tainos there giving answers he seemed to want, led him to conclude that he was not on Cipango but in Cathay: What else could that place be but the Asian mainland, and that meant somewhere near lived the Grand Khan and his fabled cities. Accordingly, Columbus sent his interpreter of Arabic and Hebrew and an able seaman along with a Lucayo pilot and a local Taino off on an inland quest for the emperor of China. They carried passports in Latin, a royal letter of introduction, and small gifts. Four days later the envoys returned. Expecting what could not be, the Christians were disappointed with the first European diplomatic mission conducted in the New World, an encounter as rich as the Cuban Tainos could provide as the redaction of Las Casas shows:

[The envoys] said that the Indians received them with great solemnity, according to their custom. And everyone came to see them, men as well as women; and they quartered them in the best houses. The Indians touched them and kissed their hands and feet, marveling and believing that the Spaniards came from the heavens, and so they gave them to understand. They gave them something to eat of what they had. The Spaniards said that upon their arrival the most honorable men of the town led them by the arm to the principal house and gave them two chairs, in which they sat; and all of them sat down on the ground around them. The Indian who went with them informed the others of the way the Christians lived and that they were good people. Later the men left, and the women came in and seated themselves in the same way around them, kissing their hands and feet and feeling them, attempting to see if they were, like themselves of flesh and bone. They begged them to stay there with them for at least five days. . . . Seeing that the Indians had no information about a city, the Spaniards returned; and if they had wanted to accommodate all who wished to come, more than 500 men and women would have come with them, because they thought that the Spaniards would return to the heavens.

Although it receives no more than a sentence, perhaps the most noteworthy occurrence happened on the trail back to the ships: "The two Christians found along the way many people going back and forth between their villages, men and women with a fire brand of weeds in their hands to take in the fragrant smoke to which they are accustomed." These words are the first indubitable European reference to tobacco. The Tainos didn't use pipes but rolled the leaves into a finger-size tube, then lighted it at one end while holding the other to a nostril; after a few inhalations the smoker passed the "cigar" to a companion or extinguished it for a later puff. Some years afterward, Las Casas would write that Spanish colonists had taken up the custom of smoking *gigarros,* and he adds, "though I don't know what taste or profit they find in it." The profit lay in another irony of Columbian exploration: The valuable herbage and spices he sent the envoys to find were not anywhere about, but literally before their noses was a plant that proved more lucrative than the gold Europeans one day would steal or extract from the Americas. In that commodity is a kind of Indian revenge, for tobacco would one day sicken and kill more Europeans and their descendants than all the natives the conquistadors laid low.

During the envoys' absence, Columbus had the *Santa María* careened, that is, hauled onto a beach so seamen could clean her hull of weeds and barnacles and cover it with fresh pitch to protect against shipworms. During that maintenance, he tried to explore the forest but found the dense vegetation made travel and observation difficult. To help gain the confidence of the Tainos, he forbade sailors to trade with them, although the crew by then probably had its fill of souvenirs and preferred to pursue Indian women whose sexual code was more free than anything they knew at home; there is, of course, no mention of such activity in the logbook, an account Queen Isabella herself would read. Columbus sampled Taino food—tubers, fruits, beans—and he showed the Indians pieces of gold, pearls, and several spices so that they could tell him where those things might be found, and each time the answer was an arm pointed east toward lands he understood to be called Babeque and Bohio, today Great Inagua and Haiti.

In one of the meetings, so says a report, Indians spoke of "one-eyed men, and others, with snouts of dogs, who ate men, and that as soon as one was taken they cut his throat and drank his blood and cut off his genitals." Because one-eyed and dog-headed men appear in the tall-story travels of the ostensible John Mandeville, these particular details suggest that Columbus was asking leading questions to prove his geographical position, and the obliging Tainos agreed. At times, accurate information they might have yielded got lost in Columbian presuppositions and bias. In this instance, it would have been useful to pursue the truth about the feared Caribs—whom the Tainos called Canibales—and their alleged cannibalism, a word that has reached us from those distant people.

Given the butchery that was about to begin in the New World, Columbus writes one passage grim with implications for American Indian culture, one important enough for Las Casas to quote him directly:

I maintain, Most Serene Princes, that if [the Indians] had access to devout religious persons knowing the language, they would all turn Christian, and so I hope in Our Lord that Your Highnesses will do something about it with much care, in order to turn to the Church so numerous a folk, and to convert them as you have destroyed those [Jews] who would not seek to confess the Father, Son, and Holy Ghost. And after your days (for we are all mortal) you will leave your realms in a very tranquil state, and free from heresy and wickedness, and will be well received before the eternal Creator.

These words, to all but those possessed of fervid messianism, must make the blood run cold of anyone who values cultural diversity and respects the right of indigenous societies to retain their unique ways. Although Columbus continually failed to comprehend it, Taino life was rich with spiritual beliefs that had maintained them for centuries, beliefs that did not urge them to force their convictions upon others or kill in the name of a deity. Their willingness to imitate uncomprehendingly the sign of the cross was not, as Columbus believed, a desire for conversion but more probably an amusement and a wish to please and show respect to the foreigners, the leader of whom—with his Queen—wanted their souls almost as much as their gold and spices.

thirteen

Over the next twenty-four days, the fleet fought wind and weather, failing to reach Great Inagua altogether, and laboring toward Haiti, although the ships were within about two hundred miles of the islands. Lured on by tales of Indians gathering gold on the beach after dark by the light of candles, Columbus zigzagged along the eastern tip of Cuba where he found several fine, natural harbors surrounded by beautiful shores and rising from them large trees and mountains. Those days were as close to a sightseeing cruise as the Europeans would have.

At the outset of that leg of the voyage, the Captain General had more Tainos captured to be taken to Spain so that they might learn Spanish to be able to reveal what they knew of their realms, and upon returning, to serve as interpreters. Columbus says:

> Yesterday there came alongside the ship a canoe with six young men in it, and when five of them entered the ship, I ordered them detained and I am bringing them. And later I sent men to a house . . . and they brought seven head of women, counting young ones and adults, and three small children. . . . I did this so that the men would behave better in Spain, having women from their country, than without them. . . . Having their women, they have a desire to carry out the business they are charged with. And also these women will teach our men much of their language. . . . There came alongside in a canoe the husband of one of these women and

the father to the three children, one male and two female; and he asked me to let him go with them and he implored me greatly: and all of them were consoled by him, for they all must be related.

We don't know what means the Spaniards used to keep the Indians captive, but the restraints were insufficient to prevent a couple of men from escaping six days later; of the others, only one or two survived to return to their homeland.

At the first landfall on Guanahani and at each subsequent place the flotilla stopped, Columbus had his sailors erect a cross; along the Oriente coast where there was considerable tall timber, the crosses became large and foreboding markers meant both to claim territory and intimidate natives. Hoping for pearls, he also had men diving for oysters, but that was as bootless as scratching for gold along beaches or in shallow rivers.

The Lucayo pilots were getting restless, and they apparently made some effort to get away, partly because they wanted to go home—as Columbus had promised if they led him to gold—and partly because the ships were nearing islands of the enemy Caribs. On the twenty-first of November, Martín Alonso Pinzón, always the thorn of Columbus, had listened to one too many Indian tales of gold to the east. Perhaps angry over not being allowed to make any personal profit, he took off without permission in *Pinta* "through cupidity," reports Las Casas who quotes Columbus: "Many other things he had done and said to me." These last words speak much about the friction between the expedition commander and one of his captains. We can see circumstantial evidence of Martín Alonso's avarice as his motivation in that his brother, Vicente Yañez, captain of *Niña*, remained with the flotilla. *Pinta* would not reappear until mid-January when Columbus was about to head home.

The only mineral the loyal Spaniards uncovered was an occasional lump of iron pyrite—fool's gold—and nowhere did they find pearls, gems, or valuable spices recognizable to a European. Nevertheless, Columbus was astute enough to predict other forms of future wealth that would involve economic and political schemes:

> It is certain, Lord Princes, that when there are such lands there should be profitable things without number. . . . Inland there must be great villages and innumerable people and things of great value; for here, and in all else that I have discovered and have hopes of discovering, before I return to Castile, I say that all Christendom will traffic with them, but most of all Spain, to which all this should be subject And I say that Your Highnesses ought not to consent that any foreigner does business or sets foot here, except Christian Catholics, since this was the end and the beginning of the enterprise.

Within these words, the last directed at keeping Jews and Muslims out of the area, are the seeds of future profits and warfare.

In that same entry, Columbus gives a remarkable detail: "Up to the present among all my people [on all ships] nobody has even had a headache or taken to his bed through sickness, except one old man . . . and he was well at the end of two days." The Captain General can take some credit for the health of his crew, but the greater part of it must go to simple good fortune, of which the first expedition had a full share.

Columbus boldly sailed near the Cuban shore that he might closely survey the bays and landscapes. With two exceptions, the explorers sent inland here and there came upon no villages the Indians hadn't abandoned minutes before, but the Christians did find large and finely made canoes, one of them big enough to hold 150 men. Passing among cultivated plots, Columbus in one village entered an emptied house he describes:

> I saw a handsome house, not very large, with two
> doors, because all of them are like that, and I went
> in and saw wonderful work like chambers made in a
> certain way that I would be unable to describe; and
> hanging from the ceiling of it [were] snail [shells?]
> and other things. I thought that it was a temple,
> and I called them and asked by signs if they said
> prayers in it. They said no. And one of them

climbed up and gave me all that there was there, and I took a bit of it.

The flight of the natives was largely a result of attacks by aggressive Caribs who raided the Cuban Indians. As the flotilla neared Haiti, Tainos aboard ship found little security even among the armed Spaniards. When the Indians realized Columbus was not to be deterred from heading there, they "couldn't speak for fear lest [Caribs] make a meal of them." To him, those fierce people had to be warriors of the Grand Khan.

At another stop, Cuban Tainos bolder than the others came down to the shore and shouted threats and waved spears, but when the Christians, armed with weapons and trinkets, got in the longboats and headed toward them, the natives disappeared. Then, six days later, after a successful trading mission, Columbus sent a detachment of seamen up a mountain to investigate what he thought was a large apiary; before his men could return, some Indians began moving toward the beached launches where the Captain General stood. A Cuban stepped into the water next to the stern and began speaking. From time to time the other Tainos raised their arms and gave loud shouts. Columbus thought they were expressing pleasure at his arrival until he saw the face of one of his Lucayo pilots "change color and become yellow as wax, and he trembled much, saying by signs that [the Europeans] had better leave the river, that [the Indians] sought to kill them." Columbus took up a sailor's cross-bow and told them the weapon could shoot far. Then he brandished a sword, and the natives took flight. It isn't clear whether Carib raids occasioned those two instances of Indian hostility or whether word had spread that the foreigners were taking captives, but the incidents were the first resistance any Indians offered the Europeans. Would the story of Spain in the Americas be different had all the early encounters been ones of armed opposition? Probably not significantly, although later history shows that aboriginal resistance often did contribute to their survival, just as it reveals across the Americas how adept Europeans were in finding ways to turn one tribe against another.

fourteen

Ill winds prevented *Santa María* and *Niña* from reaching Great Inagua, a fortuitous blow that kept Columbus away from that small island far less fruitful than Haiti on the western end of Hispaniola where the fleet headed instead. Had he followed his deepest urge of reaching the Orient by sailing westward rather than hunting commodities, he might have found gold in abundance and also much sooner come upon the answer to the question about a passage to the Indian Ocean. Although he was beginning to have suspicions that Cuba was not part of the Asian mainland, he did not modify his conviction that Cathay and the farther Indies lay not too distant.

As the ships sailed along the northwest coast of Haiti, the sailors fished with nets for edible species so plentiful one critter even jumped into a longboat. The Spaniards observed more cultivated plots but no villages, and on hilltops they saw Indian beacon fires, apparently signals warning of the foreigners' approach; in each place the fleet anchored for inland exploration, the Haitian Tainos fled before the Christians.

But on December twelfth the sailors managed to catch a woman "very young and pretty," attired in nought but a small golden nose plug. So that she might serve as an ambassador of goodwill, Columbus had her brought aboard *Santa María* and clothed—presumably in sailor's worn garments—and decorated with beads, bells, and brass rings before the seamen rowed her ashore, where-upon she indicated she wanted to go back aboard to stay with the Taino women; from this we can guess that Spanish treatment of those captives was not then so horrific as to frighten her. But the Christians sent her off homeward.

The next day nine Spaniards and a Taino followed a trail to a village of a thousand houses, where the natives again took flight. Running after them, the interpreter shouted, "The white men aren't Canibales! They carry gifts!" Perhaps the maiden's return helped, because more than two thousand Indians came back, and their leaders, though trembling, placed their hands upon Spanish heads as a sign of friendship and reverence—or so the Christians interpreted it. With fears allayed, the Haitians went into their houses and brought forth fish and casava bread, and when they learned Columbus liked parrots, out came birds. Over the next several days, the Tainos gave away so many birds the ships must have been aflitter with wings and resounding with squawks. Then, carried on the shoulders of men including her husband, came the same beautiful maiden the mariners had decked out the day before, to give thanks for what she had comprehended only as their courteous treatment. In another piece of Columbian luck, she proved to be a cacique's daughter. The first meeting on Hispaniola, the island that would one day hold the ashes of Columbus, had gone fabulously well.

The Spaniards found these people, dwellers in a beautiful valley, to be even more handsome than other Tainos they had met. Columbus did not witness any of this encounter. For unexplained reasons, he usually sent a detachment ashore while he remained aboard the flagship; as *the* crucial member of the expedition, perhaps he was protecting his safety.

By this time he had learned how to conduct a successful first encounter, and it is only his later history that makes these initial, amicable, and touching meetings lamentable in retrospect, for Columbus from the beginning possessed the ulterior motive of pacifying Indians so they might yield gold and other valuables before becoming Christianized and turned into servants and slaves. After one especially warm gathering, a shared

meal aboard *Santa María,* when it was all over Columbus
could write:

> May Your Highnesses believe that . . . this island and
> all the others are as much yours as Castile; for noth-
> ing is lacking except settlement and ordering the
> Indians to do whatever Your Highnesses may wish.
> Because I with the people that I bring with me, who
> are not many, go about in all these islands without
> danger; for I have already seen three of these sailors
> go ashore where there was a crowd of these Indians,
> and all would flee without the Spaniards wanting to
> do harm. They do not have arms and they are all
> naked, and of no skill in arms, and so very cowardly
> that a thousand would not stand against three. And
> so they are fit to be ordered about and made to
> work, plant, and do everything else that may be
> needed, and build towns and be taught our customs,
> and to go about clothed.

For someone who knows only the schoolchild myth of
Columbus, these words are shocking. Even his frequent
admirer, Las Casas, in his *History of the Indies,* found
them so:

> Note here, that the natural, simple and kind gentle-
> ness and humble condition of the Indians, and
> want of arms or protection gave the Spaniards the

insolence to hold them of little account, and to impose on them the harshest tasks that they could, and to become glutted with oppression and destruction. And sure it is that here the Admiral enlarged himself in speech more than he should, and that what he here conceived and set forth from his lips, was the beginning of the ill usage he afterwards inflicted upon them.

As for the docility of the native peoples and their willingness to be turned into chattels once they understood that the Christians were not from the sky, they would give another answer at the post Columbus would soon build on Hispaniola.

fifteen

Precious metal continued to drive the Spaniards on, especially when they heard native reports about an island composed of more gold than soil. But one cacique—showing untypical shrewdness and perhaps also doubt about the heavenly origin of the white men—picked up a golden ornament the size of his hand and disappeared into a house, only soon to reemerge offering broken bits of gold, the better to barter it. More commonly Indians outdid themselves in readily yielding all they had: food, parrots, spears and arrows, lucre. Most generously of all, the men of Haiti did not hide away women as had happened in

other places, a circumstance carrying its requisite consequences.

The nature of these various exchanges comes out in a
loaded journal redaction by Las Casas—who, we must
remember, was a Spaniard—describing the sailors' arrival
in a village, a trip that saw the Indians piggybacking the
mariners across streams and muddy places:

> When they arrived the Christians took the [cacique]
> by the hand to the [secretary of Columbus], who
> was one of those whom [Columbus] sent to forbid
> the others to do any unjust thing to the Indians.
> The Indians were so open and the Spaniards so
> greedy and disorderly that it was not enough for
> them that for a lace-end, and even for bits of glass
> and of pottery and other things of no account, the
> Indians give them all they want; but even without
> giving the Indians something, the Spaniards want to
> have and take everything, which [Columbus] always
> prohibited. . . . But [he], seeing the openhearted-
> ness of the Indians, who for six glass beads would
> give and do give a piece of gold, for that reason
> ordered that nothing should be received from them
> without giving them something in payment.

Such Taino generosity and goodwill were nearing
their acme as the first Christmas in the New World
approached. That their beneficent behavior was fully

in accord with the most holy of Christian celebrations, the natives had no notion. On December twenty-fourth, as if the spirit of the season were filling him, Columbus says:

In all the world there can be no better or gentler people. . . . Both people and land are in such quantity that I don't know how to write it. For I have spoken in superlative degree [of] the folk and country of *Juana,* which they call Cuba, but there is as much difference among them and between these and the others as between day and night. Nor do I believe that anyone else who has seen this would have done or said less than I have said and done. It is true that the things here are marvelous, and the great towns of this island Espanola (for so I called it, and they call it *Bohio*), and all show the most singular loving behavior and speak kind, not like the others who it seems when they speak are making threats; and they are of good height, men and women, and not black. It is true that all dye themselves, some with black and others with different colors, most of them with red (I have learned that they do this on account of the sun that it may not harm them so much); and the houses and villages are so fair and with government in all, such as judge or lord thereof, and all obey him so that it is a marvel. All these lords are men of few words and fair manners; and their command is [effected] more by signs of the hand, and it is understood, which is wonderful.

Columbus set those words down in the final entry before the voyage would change in a way he had known to be a constant threat since the first landfall ten weeks earlier. At last, the luck of the First Voyage was to run out nearly with the stroke of midnight marking Christmas Day. For a man dedicatedly determined to force Christianity onto an entire people, we can wonder what such an omen meant to him.

sixteen

Two days and nights of continual visits from the Tainos left Columbus and the crew of *Santa María* exhausted as they tried to sail on along the north Haitian coast against more infelicitous winds. The ships gained only a few leagues, but conditions eased as the fleet of two reached what is today Cap Haitien. For the first time, the Captain General had some knowledge of his course, which he had gained by sending sailors ahead in a launch. With *Niña* leading the way over a calm sea, a tired Columbus an hour before midnight entrusted the easy passage to the officer of the watch, Juan de La Cosa, who, improperly, soon turned his responsibility over to the helmsman, who, improperly, turned the big and clumsy tiller over to an apprentice seaman as tired as the others. Forty Europeans and the Indian captives lay sleeping.

Directly after the turn of the sandglass at midnight, in the first hour of Christmas, *Santa María* leisurely, almost imperceptibly, rode onto a coral reef not far offshore. The groggy apprentice probably felt it only in the tiller. He called out that something was wrong. Columbus was there first, soon followed by La Cosa, and the rest of the startled sailors. Sleep for that night was done. The Captain General ordered the launch, then in tow, to carry ahead an anchor into deep water so that the flagship might be kedged off the reef. La Cosa and some of his Basque countrymen went into the longboat and rowed away but not with setting the anchor in mind. Instead, trying to save themselves, they hurried toward *Niña*. Her captain, the reliable Pinzón—Vicente Yañez—ordered them to return to *Santa María*.

Fighting time, Columbus ordered the mainmast cut down to reduce weight, but nothing could save her now. The surf turned her broadside and was lifting and dropping helpless *María* repeatedly on the jagged coral that punched through her planking and admitted water into the hull. One of the most renowned ships in all history was doomed.

Based upon the evidence, much of it from Columbus himself, his lone error was to entrust La Cosa in easy wind and water, seemingly a sound decision, given that the subordinate was both master and part owner of

Santa María. Then, instead of responsibility and loyalty, La Cosa worsened things by responding to the reefing with cowardice and rank insubordination, but Columbus uses a single word to describe La Cosa's action that endangered the entire expedition—treachery.

We can surmise the thoughts of men and officers alike: How will forty extra sailors fit on little *Niña* for the return home? And what if *she* should founder? The exploration, so well executed up to that first hour of Christmas 1492, suddenly was in danger of coming to an end in a place utterly unknown in Europe. If Columbus failed to reach Spain again, how long would it be before anyone else would muster enough nerve, money, and crew to sail off onto an ocean that does not return its dead?

The men of the flagship crowded aboard *Niña* until dawn. Then, in a darkness of heart and mind unlike anything they'd yet experienced, the sailors began the arduous work of salvaging what they could, having to chop holes in the *Holy Mary* to get out her stores. Columbus sent an envoy ashore to ask help from the Taino cacique, Guacanagari, who quickly responded with all his canoes and many people. Las Casas writes that the chief also sent a relative to the weeping Columbus to tell him "that he should not be sorrowful or annoyed because [Guacanagari] would give him all that he had." Before night fell on that Christmas, the salvageable goods were onshore under watch of sailors and Tainos. Not so much as a nail was taken.

The Indians, whom Columbus had only recently described as typically given to joyful laughter, wept with him. Their sympathy and openheartedness moved him to say, "They love their neighbors as themselves." If there are any words in the logbook of Christopher Columbus to bear in mind from this point forward in his history, these are the ones.

The first Christmas in the Americas was celebrated not with self-righteous piety and idle ceremony, but with a practical expression of those guiding and encompassing eleven words of the Golden Rule. Given the subsequent actions of Europeans in the New World, apparently no Christian was listening, although the irony would not escape Bishop Las Casas who, in a marginal note in the journal, writes of his own countrymen: "Observe the humanity of the Indians toward the tyrants who have exterminated them." Anyone today who argues that we should not judge Columbus—and those to follow him— by our modern moral standards plainly overlooks Las Casas and his contemporaries who knew the future Admiral of the Ocean Sea just as they also knew slavery was evil.

seventeen

The long journal entry for the day after Christmas is the most startling and revealing in the entire logbook. With his flagship gone, the voyage of discovery deeply imperiled, how did Columbus respond? With more tears, depression, anger, punishment for the malefactors?

At sunrise, Guacanagari visited *Niña,* now become the flagship, to cheer his Spanish friend. While they talked, Tainos from another village, unaware of the disaster, paddled up, stood in their canoe, and showed pieces of gold, all the while imitating the sound of hawk bells, their most desired item. Columbus smiled at the renewed promise of wealth to be gained for next to nothing, and his spirits rose yet further when Guacanagari told him he knew where there was so much gold the Christians could have all they wanted.

Columbus asked the good cacique to dine aboard *Niña* and gave him a shirt (as much to cover his nakedness as a gift) and gloves, the latter bringing him unbounded pleasure. When they finished, Guacanagari invited his friend ashore for a native feast of lobster, game, casava bread, and other viands. At the conclusion, the cacique washed his hands vigorously and rubbed them with herbs. Filled and content, the men took a tour with a thousand naked people excitedly following along the beach where the leaders' talk turned to enemy raids on the Tainos. We can question with what accuracy ideas passed from one language into the other, but wishing to reward Guacanagari, Columbus ordered a display of archery and cannons, explosions that sent the Indians diving for cover, and he promised that the great powers in far-off Castile would order enemy Caribs destroyed.

Then the Tainos brought forth what has to be one of the most perspicacious, if unintended, symbols in all the histories of the Americas. To the man hiding his plan of enslavement, a leader who now could see only auric metal and would listen only to tales about it, a captain blind and deaf, the Indians gave a large mask with gold for eyes and ears. Las Casas says that Columbus "received much pleasure and consolation from these things that he saw; and the anguish and sorrow that he had received and felt because of the loss of the ship were tempered; and he recognized that Our Lord had caused the ship to ground there so that he would found a settlement there."

Then the Bishop quotes this illuminating entry by Columbus:

> It is certain . . . that if I had not gone aground I would have passed at a distance without anchoring at this place, because it is located here inside a large bay, and in it [there are] two or three reefs and shoals; nor on this voyage would I have left people here; nor, even if I had wished to leave them, could I have given them such good supplies or so many tools or so much foodstuff or equipment for a fortress. And it is quite true that many [crewmen] of those who are here have begged me and have had others beg me to be willing to give them license to stay. Now I have ordered them to build a tower and a fort, all very well constructed, and a big moat, not

that I believe it to be necessary because of these
Indians, for it is obvious that with the men that I
bring I could subdue all of this island, which I
believe is larger than Portugal and double or more
in [number of] people, since they are naked and
without arms and cowardly beyond remedy.

Content indeed is the mind that can take disaster and
turn it into predestined good fortune, and convenient it
was, at a stroke, to solve the most serious and pressing
problem of what to do with forty extra seamen on a ship
that needed a crew only half that number. Given the
splendid anchorages Columbus had recently seen, it still
apparently never occurred to him to question why the
Divine Plan picked out such a poor and ultimately disas-
trous one.

To him, the failure to save the *Holy Mary* would now
mean salvation of thousands of heathen souls. Of course,
because those souls were savage—that is, "of the
woods"—they would never receive the opportunity to
decide for themselves whether they wanted "deliverance" or to be taught to mouth a Golden Rule they
already were practicing.

This remarkable, if chilling, logbook entry concludes
with Columbus setting out his plan for the colonial outpost of La Navidad, the Holy Nativity, named to honor a
day on which he considered was born a great and good
disaster. There on his return he hoped to find a cask full

of gold, the source of the metal, and enough valuable spices to underwrite a new war on the Muslims who still held the Holy Sepulcher. Columbus says, "All the gain of this my Enterprise should be spent in the conquest of Jerusalem."

eighteen

Wanting to make the most of the loss of *Santa María*, Columbus set his mariners—using Indians for heavy work—to constructing the small fortress out of her timbers, planks, and hardware, while he prepared for the return to Spain in *Niña*. With Martín Pinzón absconded and only a single ship remaining, further exploration was too risky, even considering reports by some Tainos that *Pinta* was not far east. On the chance she might be, the Commander sent a seaman, guided by an Indian in a canoe, with a letter, typical of Columbian practicality and diplomacy, expressing hope Pinzón would return.

Columbus continued inquiring about the location of the gold mines, but language problems—and maybe also a native reluctance to divulge all—kept him from learning much that was accurate. Even the friendly Guacanagari seemed to dissemble on that point, perhaps to ensure that all gold would pass through him. Whenever Columbus mentions Indian innocence, he doesn't mean stupidity. The jolly cacique showered more metallic gifts on his new friend and even promised a life-size golden statue of him if he would stay long enough for it to be made. Columbus, at last, presented to Guacanagari a few things worth more than a brass hawk bell: taking it from his own neck, he placed an agate necklace around the cacique who had rendered him critical aid; then the Commander gave him a big silver ring, a fine red cape, and high-laced shoes. Two other Taino leaders responded with a pair of large pieces of flattened gold. Spanish-Indian relations were again going well.

Captain Vicente Yañez Pinzón said he had seen rhubarb sprouting, a potentially important find. The root of Chinese rhubarb, a relative of the American kind, when carried to Europe by caravan, brought a high price as a medicinal powder; to Columbus, who knew Marco Polo's reference to it, rhubarb was further proof that the fleet was indeed in Asia. One plant the Captain General might have paid greater attention to— he mentions little more than the Indians found it wholesome and wouldn't eat without it—was capsicum; chile pepper in one form or another would soon sweep over the Eastern Hemisphere as black pepper did Europe. The Tainos called it *axi*. Columbus says he could load fifty ships a year with it, but then doesn't speak of it again.

Were it were true that *Pinta* was nearby, he knew he must beat the deserters back to Spain to protect his own interests and prevent Pinzón from poisoning the minds of Ferdinand and Isabella against him. When fortress La Navidad was complete enough, he went ashore to say farewell to Guacanagari and took the opportunity to display Spanish power—whether to be used against the feared Caribs *or* any Tainos who might get dangerous ideas—by ordering the post cannons to fire shots through the remains of *Santa María;* to further his message, he even staged mock combat among armed seamen. Clearly his announcement was: We can defend you, or we can destroy you.

Thirty-nine men from both crews apparently volunteered to stay among the warm and garbless Taino women and hunt gold around La Navidad—now provided with ship's artillery, weapons, a longboat, enough bread and biscuit for a year, wine, seeds for sowing, and most of the remaining trade trinkets.

On January 4, 1493, a favorable wind came on at last, and *Niña* set out eastward along the northern coast of Haiti toward what is today the border with the Dominican Republic. Progress was slow. Two days later, Columbus sent a sailor up the high mainmast to watch for shoals, but what he saw was something else. In the distance he could make out the sails of *Pinta*. After an absence of forty-seven days, Martín Pinzón drew close to the new flagship; in the meeting that followed he excused himself by saying he had departed against his will. Exactly what he meant is unclear, although most improbable. Columbus, keeping his own counsel out of the practical necessity of needing the added security of a sister ship for the long return, believed Pinzón was prevaricating. The truth lay in the captain's quest for gold, which he apparently did find on Hispaniola, keeping half for himself, dividing the remainder among his crew. Columbus writes, "I shall not suffer the deeds of lewd fellows devoid of virtue, who contrary to him who conferred honor upon them, presume to do their own will, with slight respect." But suffer them he did.

Relations between the two men, whose motives were not so dissimilar on the question of New World gold, must have been tensely difficult and workable only out of the need for their mutual safe return home. The single action the Commander took against Pinzón was to release six Indians Martín had captured, while keeping those of his own abductions and impressing four more a couple of days later.

But all things were not worrisome. The men caught some sea turtles to add to their plates, and Columbus says he saw three mermaids rise high from the waves. Recognizing the similarity of those manatees to dugongs he'd seen on the west coast of Africa, he writes a sentence as close to humor as he can express when he says the "mermaids were not as beautiful as they are painted, although to some extent they have a human appearance in the face." But Columbus *was* credulous about native stories telling of an all-woman island lying to the south that seemed to coincide with Marco Polo's assertion that such a place existed in the Indian Ocean, further proof to Columbus he had reached the Indies. This ancient myth of the Amazons would eventually lead to the naming of the New World's largest river, one Vicente Yañez Pinzón would soon introduce to Europe.

On the thirteenth of January, Columbus came upon his final encounter with Indians, but these people were not like those he had met earlier. He considered this tribe not as handsome as the Tainos. They spoke a somewhat different tongue and painted themselves a charcoal black, wore their hair long and bound behind with parrot feathers; they carried bows and arrows, the first the Christians had seen among the Indians. Most significantly, they were aggressive, less easily intimidated, and not possessed of any notion that the foreigners hailed from the heavens. Columbus took them to be the feared and nearly fearless Caribs. After luring one of them aboard *Niña* and giving him the usual truck, Columbus sent him and seven sailors to shore where the Indian coaxed his friends to put down their weapons and come forward. The Europeans, by order, began trading for bows and arrows in an attempt to disarm them, but the natives, becoming suspicious, gave up only a couple of bows before running for ones they had earlier laid down; then they turned on the seven seamen in what seemed an attack. During the ensuing melee, a Christian slashed open the buttocks of one Indian and another sailor shot an arrow into a native's chest. With that, the Indians retreated, and it took an order from the master of the longboat to prevent more bloodshed.

The mariners woke the next morning to find many people on the shore, but they had come for barter, not battle. When the Europeans reached shore they saw the man they'd given the trinkets to standing near a cacique bearing gifts of shell beads. Columbus asked him and his small retinue aboard *Niña* for a parley that went so pleasantly the Carib promised to send a golden mask along with gifts of cotton, bread, and yams to the visitors. The next day he fulfilled his pledge, and relations, driven by force, again seemed amicable.

This first serious Christian–Indian skirmish, occurring at the very last anchorage the flotilla would make in the Americas on that initial voyage, then appeared only an aberration. What had begun peaceably on Guanahani ended with harmonious exchanges boding well for the future. Before dawn on the following morning, January sixteenth, the two caravels, their crews reduced nearly by half, set out for home ninety-six days after first stepping ashore in the Americas.

nineteen

On the first leg of the homebound voyage, Columbus intended to follow his Indian pilots' directions southward to the "island of women," not so much out of curiosity as to find stronger evidence than he yet had that he was indeed in the Indies. To land on Marco Polo's Island Feminea and bring home a few captives could furnish such proof. But the wind shifted against the flotilla and Columbus gave up his plan and headed for Spain, or, rather, headed where he thought Spain was. Had winds allowed him to sail that route, the one he initially believed correct, he likely would have missed the entire Iberian Peninsula and ended up west of Ireland.

He had no knowledge of the great North Atlantic gyre, that circling of winds and currents moving generally clockwise: to reach the West Indies from southern Spain, a ship should sail a slightly curving course from the three o'clock position to eight o'clock; to return, it does not repeat the outward-bound heading but proceeds in an arcing route northeasterly to nine o'clock and, more or less, continues on around to come again to three. A decade later, when Columbus made his last voyage, mariners were beginning to understand the gyration of the Ocean Sea.

The fleet sailed northerly to about the latitude of Bermuda and then turned east where the ships caught strong winter westerlies that propelled them smartly toward home. Among the many discoveries that Columbus made but had no accurate conception of, this route east, a necessity for sailing ships, was another, just as it was one more instance of Columbian luck coinciding with his shrewdness as a navigator. He did not, however, see it as luck; to him it was further manifestation of his divinely

granted destiny. Even the loss of *Santa María* helped him, for she would have slowed the swifter caravels.

With fair winds and gently rolling seas, the ships slipped through the cooling air and water as they headed again into uncharted ocean. All hands took cheer in the schools of tuna that seemed to tow them homeward. To replenish the much-diminished food stores—by then down to bread, wine, and Hispaniola yams—the sailors caught a porpoise and a large shark. With a following sea, life was good. The men could fish, toy with their souvenirs, tell tales of Indian women, and even rest and whittle as they watched the leagues slip behind, sometimes at an almost phenomenal ten knots. The only annoyance were the occasional slowings to let *Pinta* with her unsound mast catch up. Had Martín Pinzón, Columbus grumbled, been as earnest to prepare his ship for sea as he was to fill it with gold, the return crossing would have been speedier yet. But this encumbrance also would eventually help Columbus by allowing him to reach Spain first and be the one to announce the great news.

For twenty-eight days, he sailed the ocean blue as sweetly as he could hope. How fine it must have been to know he carried what was now the greatest, most valuable bit of geographical knowledge in all of Europe. Keeping much of his navigational data to himself (and giving more false positions on that homeward leg), he was perhaps the only man alive with detailed sailing instructions for the western route to his Indies. He

believed he had proved all his opponents and mockers wrong, fulfilled his mission to the Crown, and rightly earned himself the promised title of Admiral of the Ocean Sea. All he needed to do was follow through, keep the capricious, self-seeking Pinzón under close watch, and hope for continued congenial wind and weather. Samuel Eliot Morison, who sailed in 1939 along the route of Columbus, mused on conditions in 1493: "February 1 was the night of the full moon, and the effect of moonlight on a sargassum-covered ocean with fresh and favoring wind impelling your ships through the undulating meadow at a high rate of speed, the weed making a peculiar soft swishing sound as it brushes by, has a strange and magical beauty." And so it went for nearly a month. Then sea and sky, wind and weather changed. The men had no idea they were sailing into one of the worst winters Europe had seen in years.

As the ships entered a tempestuous area of the North Atlantic, an intense low-pressure cell was stirring winds to gale force and creating opposing waves that formed into big and dangerous pyramids, a shape to send fear into the stoutest mariner. With the wooden ships pitching and rolling, their masts bare of sail, the captains had to give their vessels over to the wind and water, and the officer of the watch could do little more than direct the helmsman toward an angle that would best take on the waves, a mostly futile exercise in those circumstances. Anyone who has been at sea under such conditions knows how

unbearably long an hour then is. The thrashing, the fearful noises, the clothes soaked by the cold Atlantic, the unceasing worry whether a seventy-foot wooden hull could withstand any more—all of those elements made sleep impossible and eating nearly so. Columbus, as bold a shellback as ever went down to the sea, says "my weakness and anxiety would not allow my spirit to be soothed."

The ships signaled with flares, but by dawn on February fourteenth, the storm had separated them, and *Pinta* was nowhere visible. Whether she was just out of sight or had gone down, no one could say. Scant as it was, the comfort of a sister ship in view vanished, so Columbus turned to celestial negotiation: Should *Niña* be spared, somebody must make a pilgrimage to Santa María de Guadalupe in the mountains of western Spain. Garbanzo beans matching the number of all Christians (Indians excluded), one of the beans marked with a cross, were dropped into a cap, shaken, and passed to the first man to draw, the Captain General himself. He reached in and, lo, pulled out the garbanzo of the cross. It's likely that no one else wanted it more or would be more faithful in fulfilling the vow.

But the tempest raged on. Soon the cap of garbanzos went around again until an ordinary seamen pulled out the marked bean that meant he had to make an even longer pilgrimage to the Shrine of Santa Maria de Loreto in Italy, one so distant Columbus promised to pay the cost of his travel. Perhaps, over the racketing storm, the heavens couldn't hear the vows of frightened and desperate sailors, because the tempest continued. Again, out came the garbanzos and once more Columbus drew the crossed bean. (The odds suggest that he rigged it or that the seamen rigged it against him.) And still the gale blew and the waves beat over *Niña*. At last, every mariner agreed to make a procession, wearing nothing but their shirts, to the first shrine dedicated to Mother Mary they came upon. But the violence went on unabated, leaving the men to pray their way into private vows and confessions because "no one thought to escape, all regarding themselves as lost."

Columbus weighed reasons his God "might wish him to perish" against those that should indicate his Grand Puissance wanted him to reach the Spanish court with his great news, the most astounding narrative Europe had heard in centuries. He worried not so much about himself as his two sons, and surely he also had to be concerned that *Pinta* might survive to allow Martín Pinzón to seize the glory and wealth, leaving his own boys nothing. His years of labor and suffering seemed about to be wasted by a single storm.

He sat down to record all that he had found, and he beseeched whomever should find his account to carry it to the Spanish throne. He wrapped the document in waxed cloth and, unbeknown to anyone else, sealed the parchment in a large wooden barrel and had it tossed into the pounding ocean he had so hoped to become admiral of. The sailors assumed his action was a devotion to save them. Perhaps a celestial skipper at last noted what was going on below and took the cask on board a ship of heaven, for the barrel hasn't been seen since—but the weather did change.

By morning, the storm moderating, Columbus beheld a further amazement: On the horizon rose a shadowy outline of some terra firma. The half-crazed pilots and sailors believed it was landlocked Castile. Columbus said it was the Azores, unfortunately the territory of Portugal, the great competitor and sometimes enemy of Spain. He was correct. The island was—yes—Santa Maria, one of the smallest in the Azores and without a good harbor. Having resigned themselves to the deeps, what relief the sailors found in that misty little hump, although finding a safe anchorage was something else. In the course of searching for one, *Niña* lost two anchors and continually had to change her position to avoid being swept onto the rocks.

That Columbus actually reached the Azores by sailing an uncharted sea with only a compass—a device of limited use when a sailor isn't precisely certain where he is starting from—testifies to his great capacities as a navigator. That he could repeatedly find his way with such comparative precision, as will become evident, proves this aspect of his seafaring was not part of the Columbian luck. Martín Pinzón, the would-be fleet commander, apparently missed the Azores by several hundred miles, even with Columbus leading the way for nearly a month.

The Captain General had gotten no sleep for three or four days during the worst of the tempest, and he'd eaten almost nothing as he stood exposed to the continual drenchings of the cold North Atlantic. His legs had become "much crippled," plausibly the onset of the infectious arthritis or a related disorder that would plague him until his death. But he was alive, and now he knew the way home.

twenty

Since the Azores were under the sovereignty of Portugal, Columbus had not intended to stop there lest he be taken for someone illegally trading along the West African coast, also Portuguese territory. But desperate *Niña* required repairs, her men needed respite, and supplies needed replenishing. At the first opportunity to fulfill the fourth storm-induced vow, Columbus sent ashore half the crew for a pilgrimage to a small chapel dedicated to the omnipresent Holy Virgin to whom they had so pleaded for intercession. Shoeless and unclothed but for their tunics—correct devotional attire for such an endeavor—the sailors boated in, formed up, and walked solemnly to the shrine, whereupon an entire village, at the orders of a young and minor official, "fell upon them and took them all prisoners."

When the supplicants did not return, Columbus moved *Niña* to a less secure anchorage but one allowing him to see the chapel before going ashore himself. As he got ready, more luck bechanced him. The young official rowed out to *Niña* and demanded to know what ship his was and why it was there. With some pomposity, the Captain General declared he was Admiral of the Ocean Sea and was returning from the Indies. The functionary must have said something on the order of, Of course you are, and I'm the King of Fairies—but you still must come ashore. Columbus understood he could be clapped into jail along with his men, and he refused to leave *Niña*. Considerable posturing and shouting followed, with the Captain General threatening to have the official punished once Columbus could return to Spain, words as incredible as his other claims. At last, in high dudgeon, he promised to "depopulate" the island were his men not returned. With that, things came to a standstill.

Needing time to see what other remedy or diplomacy he might effect, Columbus gave orders to weigh anchor, and *Niña* moved off. He might have foreseen then that his four returns to Europe would not be all triumph gratefully received by Court or commoners. When he came back for his men two days later, Columbus found the official, apparently convinced there had been no illegal trading in Guinea, ready to release the sailors. With his crew restored, he went to find water and wood for the final leg home, still some 800 miles distant. He'd spent ten days in the Azores, time enough for Martín Pinzón, were he still alive, to reach Spain ahead of him and steal his thunder.

On the twenty-fourth of February, *Niña* once more set out for blue water. Three days later nasty weather struck again, and the caravel wallowed in the pounding of a storm worse than the one they just escaped. Las Casas echoes Columbus, "It was very painful to have such a tempest when they were already at the doors of home." The foul winds wracked the ship, eventually splitting her sails, and a second time the sailors gave themselves up to doom, their only defense another passing of the garbanzos for yet another pilgrimage. Columbus, of course, "won" it. With *Niña* crippled, he had to employ every bit of his nautical skills, all of his resoluteness, and each degree of his courage: He knew the wind was driving *Niña* toward the rocky coast of Portugal, and a sailing ship without canvas is helpless. Waves crashed in two directions over the decks, a fearsome thing indeed, and lightning struck from every point of the compass, and the gale "seemed to raise the caravel into the air." Such conditions negate any execution of shipmanship, for in seas like those a sailor survives by his good luck or by his God.

Just after dark on the third of March the answer arrived. The sky began to open, and enough moonlight allowed the mariners to make out a hard coast in the distance, not good news given their impotence. Columbus ordered the last spare sail to be brought up, and, in the lessening blow, the sailors "with infinite toil and terror" hoisted it and managed to keep *Niña* off the rocks until dawn. When he went to the rail at first light, Columbus recognized the steep cliffs just west of Lisbon. Because he could do nothing else, he made for the Portuguese city, aware the great rival of Spain might have notions to do him in. As the beaten and bedraggled *Niña* made her way up the Tagus estuary, the sight of the poor vessel moved fishermen, having no idea where she had come from, to cross themselves.

On Monday morning, the fourth of March, Columbus called out to drop anchor just south of the heart of Lisbon, coincidentally at the place where today rest the bones of his great contemporary mariner, Vasco da Gama. To protect himself from any Portuguese mischief, and to try to preempt Pinzón, and to reassure his Sovereigns that he was in Lisbon harbor only out of necessity, he dispatched letters: one to the King of Portugal to explain his reason for being there, and another to Ferdinand and Isabella to give a précis of his Enterprise of the Indies.

Soon a Portuguese official approached *Niña* to demand Columbus come ashore and give explanations, but, knowing the risk, he refused, although he was as powerless as a commander can be. He could only show his papers and repeat his incredible claim of returning from the Orient. His resoluteness and skills of persuasion once again served him. A higher government official finally came to *Niña* and, with much ceremony, welcomed him. There seemed nothing Columbus couldn't escape.

Four days later the King of Portugal, who had twice turned down the Enterprise, invited him to visit the court some thirty miles north of Lisbon. Several versions of the meeting exist. Columbus said he was treated with all respect, but others wrote that he spoke above his station and irritated the King, who was further annoyed at having missed being the recipient of the newly discovered realm with its rich promise. Everyone agrees there was no foul play, and Columbus, after stopping off to see the Portuguese Queen and give his report a second time, returned safely to his ship. By then, his account must have been taking on some polish.

With her sails replaced, *Niña* went down the tidal river and started toward Palos on the thirteenth of March. Columbus had dodged another threat to the completion of his voyage. As he changed course to the east at Cape Saint Vincent, he must have remembered how (according to one story) seventeen years earlier he used an oar to buoy himself and swam ashore to survive a sinking ship. The landing he was about to make, despite his battered and sorry caravel, would be different. After waiting for the flood tide on March 15, 1493, he crossed the bar of the Saltés River and entered the haven that had witnessed his departure seven and half months before. Those 224 days had changed history everywhere forever.

twenty-one

The anchors of *Niña* were hardly set when her sailors looked up to see, in a coincidence of timing, *Pinta* coming up in their wake. Martín Pinzón, a mediocre navigator, had sailed north after the first tempest separated the caravels, and although *Pinta* reached Spain before her sister ship (just as she was first to espy the New World), Pinzón arrived far to the north, near Vigo. From there he sent word to the Crown, then at Barcelona, of his return and requested an audience to tell of his discoveries. Ferdinand and Isabella replied they would wait to hear it from Columbus himself, further evidence that Pinzón was never the true leader of the expedition. The additional time he spent sailing too far north and the delay of waiting for the royal response allowed the rightful man, by only a bowsprit, to reach home port first. Martín Alonso, worn down by the rigors of travel and perhaps deflated by the regal snubbing, never contested Columbus further. The exhausted Pinzón went to his home near where *Pinta* lay at anchor and, in a matter of days, died. The triumph of Columbus belonged solely to him.

From Palos all the way to the royal court in Barcelona, Columbus found himself celebrated and fêted. The amazing news out of Portugal and Spain spread rapidly to Italy, then more slowly into northern Europe, passed along, through the so-called Barcelona (or Santangel) Letter allegedly from Columbus himself. There was, of course, that one bugaboo of a detail: He had not, as he said, reached Asia. Still holding his view of a narrow Atlantic, he missed few opportunities to remind former detractors and mockers of their doubting his enterprise; nevertheless, the most informed of them continued to believe Ptolemy's estimate of the size of the earth was much closer than the smaller figure Columbus calculated, and that meant, wherever else he'd traveled, it couldn't have been to Asia. But just then that didn't matter. The full truth and proof of the question would not be settled until twenty-nine years later when Magellan's expedition circumnavigated the globe.

Columbus struck out overland for Barcelona with a small entourage including the six Tainos, each dressed, at least for ceremonies, in native costume. Whatever they thought of the wondrous sights they beheld, we have no record. Christopher stopped along the way in Cordoba to visit his two sons and the mother of the younger one; of that meeting we have no record either, but the boys must have sat enthralled hearing stories from the mouth of one of the greatest adventurers in all of history, their father.

Enthralled also, but by golden objects and assurances of rich mines and by the exotically feathered and decorated Indians, were Ferdinand and Isabella who conferred the promised title of "Admiral of the Ocean Sea, Viceroy and Governor of the Islands that he has discovered in the Indies." They asked Columbus to advise them on the major issue of securing Spanish title to the new lands and ones yet to come to light. Almost immediately, the King and Queen managed to get Pope Alexander VI, a Spaniard indebted to them for various favors, to issue four papal bulls setting forth the right of Spain to territories lying west of a line extending from the Azores to the Canary Islands. The result was manifestly unfair to Portugal, whose king was already working to equip a westward expedition. Nevertheless, through a most effective piece of diplomacy, the two nations a year later resolved differences with a treaty that divvied up the new realms in a way that proved comparatively frictionless over the succeeding years.

Ferdinand and Isabella desired that Columbus begin at once to prepare for a Second Voyage, one of colonization. The Admiral drew up a western settlement plan that, above all, tried to lay out methods to control the gathering of gold, something he understood would be the keenest motivation for colonists. In this first attempt to set down European rules for the New World, Columbus included for himself a percentage on all gold brought into Spain, a sum in addition to one previously agreed to; had the Crown honored the first contract or accepted the second, Columbus soon would have become one of the richest men in Europe. But even as it was, in middle age, he could have retired to wealth and the glory then at its height and left the dangers and privations of exploration to others. But he wanted something more, something that would alter his honorable reputation which he then still deserved: Columbus wanted to bring, as converts or chattels, the people in all the lands he would discover into a Spanish Christendom that had just expelled perhaps almost half a million Jews from the country and burned thousands of men and women whose views fanatical inquisitors found heretical.

Following the final entry in the first logbook of Columbus, Spanish bishop Bartolomé de Las Casas adds his own postscript alluding to the hope the new Admiral expresses in his last sentence that his Enterprise of the Indies "will be to the greater glory of Christianity." Having seen the subsequent work of the conquistadors play out in the following years, Las Casas writes: "Carnal men have not appreciated the benefits spiritual and temporal that God offered Spain; but Spain by her ambition and cupidity was not worthy to enjoy the spiritual ones." And it's there the story leads next.

The Second Voyage

one

The Second Voyage of Columbus was a considerably different undertaking from the First. No longer was exploration the paramount goal; now the heart of the plan was establishment of a trading colony on a scale not yet seen in Europe, not even in Portuguese West Africa. But the *declared* primary purpose was something else—forcing Indians into the ecclesiastical power of Spain and Rome. The first formal step in that direction went well with the baptisms of the six Tainos Columbus brought back, although they, innocent of Christian theology, likely interpreted the ceremony as a mere honor rather than a relinquishing of their own native spiritual beliefs. It should surprise no one, however, that despite the several holy fathers assigned to accompany the physical appurtenances for building a church in Hispaniola, missionary zeal never overcame the professed secondary reason for

95

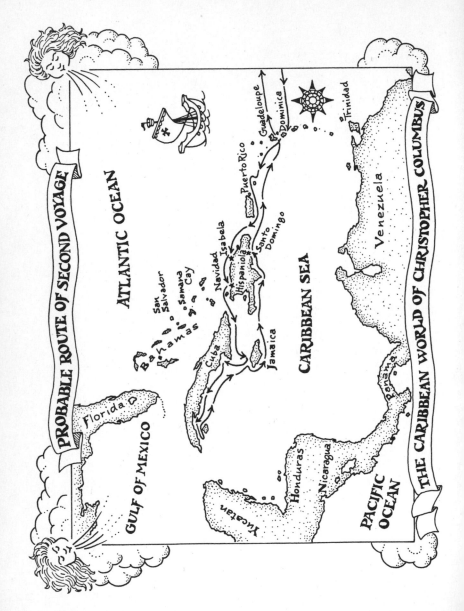

PROBABLE ROUTE OF SECOND VOYAGE

THE CARIBBEAN WORLD OF CHRISTOPHER COLUMBUS

ATLANTIC OCEAN

GULF OF MEXICO

Florida

Bahamas

San Salvador

Samana Cay

Cuba

Navidad

Isabela

Hispaniola

Santo Domingo

Puerto Rico

Guadeloupe

Dominica

Trinidad

Venezuela

CARIBBEAN SEA

Jamaica

Yucatan

Honduras

Nicaragua

Panama

PACIFIC OCEAN

the colony. That it took six years to lure the first convert suggests the urgent motivation was not God, but gold.

No journal by Columbus or any redaction of his log-book for the 1493 voyage survives, but other sources, letters and documents, are rather numerous if brief. What is not abundant are words from Columbus himself. On the new journey, we hear far more about him than from him, something one must consider in any interpretation of his deeds.

The intention was for a round-trip voyage of six months with seventeen vessels, three of them larger than anything Columbus had at his command the first time. The new flagship, another *Santa María,* this one nick-named *Maríagalante,* was noticeably bigger than the *não* that left her timbers on the Haitian reef. Twelve of the remaining craft were smaller caravels, one of them the doughty *Niña* herself; if *Pinta* was there also, we have no record of her. The rest of the fleet was probably a few small vessels suitable for shoal waters and estuary explorations. The Crown paid for the ships with money expropriated from expelled Jews.

On board were more than a thousand men—volunteers were legion across Spain—but no women, for their role as settlers was yet to come. Both the crew and the colonizers composed of craftsmen and laborers, hailed mostly from the area around Palos, but several sailors hailed from Genoa, including Columbus's childhood chum, Michele de Cuneo, whose long and lively letter about the voyage is a key source for details. Unlike the full crew list of the initial expedition, only a scattering of other names remains for this trip, but one that does is young Ponce de León who later would accomplish something his Admiral never did—become the first Spaniard to set foot in what is today the continental United States. Of the six Tainos, all were aboard except for one who stayed in Spain to become part of the royal household. Besides Cuneo, Columbus had another person whom he could trust: his youngest brother, Diego. Las Casas describes him as "peaceable and simple, and of good disposition, neither artful nor mischievous, who went very modestly clothed in a sort of clerical garb." Of greater capacities and more useful to the expedition commander, as we shall see, would have been his other brother, Bartholomew, who was working in France when the fleet sailed.

On that day, September 25, 1493, the Admiral of the Ocean Sea was not well, but he must have made his way topside to see the pageantry of the departure of his fleet, described by him as "so united and handsome," a farewell remarkably different from the one thirteen months earlier; this time there were booming cannons, blaring trumpets, an escort of bright Venetian galleys, and enough flying pennants, crested banners, and royal standards that the flags got entangled in the ships' riggings. The port of embarkation was not the plain village of Palos but, sixty miles down the coast, handsome Cadiz, a walled city founded by those ancient masters of maritime, the Phoenicians. Cadiz was about to become the European emporium for the Americas, and into her harbor over the subsequent years would arrive wealth almost beyond measure.

The Admiral—and again Commander of the Fleet—alert for any Portuguese interference, set his course once more toward the Canary Islands where the ships stopped only long enough to reprovision and take aboard live animals—kept penned on the open decks—suitable for a mining and agricultural settlement. By Sunday, the thirteenth of October, a year and a day from the first landfall on Guanahani, the flotilla escaped the Canary calms, and although La Navidad was the destination, Columbus followed a southwest heading he hoped would lead to yet more islands new to Europeans. If the Ocean Sea was still very much unknown water, it was no longer entirely uncharted, although for a time yet, only one man knew the precise sailing directions to the New World.

two

By questioning his Taino pilots as best he could, given the language difficulties, Columbus was able to lay out such an excellent transatlantic course that his seventeen ships crossed the nearly three thousand miles between the western Canaries and the second landfall in only twenty-one days. (The storm-beset *Mayflower*, about a century later, took more than two months to reach America, and she missed her intended destination by nearly five hundred miles.) For the second Columbian voyage, there was only one gale, a blow far less disruptive than any of the tempests of the previous February, and after the ships were beyond the Canary calms, they enjoyed a steady wind day and night. This fair passage was a consequence of more luck: Delays in assembling the expedition in Cadiz kept the fleet in port until the Caribbean hurricane season had passed. Still, the crossing might have been even quicker were it not for the slowness of the heavy flagship; nevertheless, *Mariagalante* would become the Admiral's favorite of all his large command vessels. The surgeon aboard her writes, "We came as straight as if we had been following a well known and customary course." The combination of the Admiral's navigational expertise, the knowledge of the Tainos, and his luck or providential destiny were all excellently effective on the Second Voyage in his sailing from Spain to the West Indies the shortest and best route, one sailing ships still follow today.

Free from fears and doubts of an uncertain crew on that trip, Columbus had to face only the more usual problems of men impatient for gold and native women. Over an ocean often as slick as a planed board, the seamen and craftsmen had time to watch flying fish and porpoises and to dream about wealth they would return home with, all the time taking comfort in the cluster of so many other sails around them. Except for the customary rigors and inconveniences of life at sea in the fifteenth century, the outward-bound leg of the Second Voyage was a delight.

On Sunday morning, the third of November, once more the cry of "*Tierra!*" rang out, this time from the flagship. Ahead lay a shadowy land the Indians called Caire but which Columbus, in honor of their arrival day, named Dominica, one of the fairest isles in the Caribbean. Like many other islands in the Leewards, it has no good harbors, so the fleet moved on to its downwind side to anchor. Repeating the formal ceremony performed on Guanahani thirteen months earlier, Columbus went ashore with suitable witnesses to claim possession for his Sovereigns. History, however, would take another course: Spain colonized only Trinidad in the Lesser Antilles, leaving the other islands to England, France, and Holland.

In that southeastern region of the Caribbean, the natives were not the peaceable and usually genial Tainos but pugnacious Caribs who preyed upon other islanders. The Spaniards began to learn how different the Caribs were the second day when the fleet hove to offshore Guadalupe, named after the shrine Columbus had recently visited to fulfill the first vow he made during the February tempest. "For the purposes of plunder," said a witness, the Admiral allowed ten sailors to go off into a forest reportedly so thick they couldn't see the sun or stars to navigate, and, directionless, they got lost. The day following, Columbus sent out two hundred men with horns and lanterns, and those teams were gone so long, their shipmates began to fear for them also. At last they came dragging back, having found nothing but weariness. After four days, with the necessity to sail onward pressing Columbus, someone at the last moment noticed a signal fire atop a peak, and the fleet moved to the nearest shore. Still, the ten men could not find their way to the beach until stumbling upon an elderly Carib woman to guide them.

In the village houses, the Christians came upon fine headdresses, earthenware pots, expertly woven cotton rugs, and the first pineapples they'd ever seen, but they turned up no gold whatsoever. Their main accomplishment was in not being eaten by those anthropophagous Caribs, for the search party entered one freshly empty village where, says Samuel Eliot Morison, the seamen "found large cuts and joints of human flesh, shinbones set aside to make arrows of, caponized [Taino] boy captives who were being fattened for the griddle, and girl captives who were mainly used to produce babies, which the Caribs regarded as a particularly toothsome morsel."

According to Columbus's friend Michele de Cuneo, the sailors brought back to the ship "twelve very beautiful and plump girls fifteen to sixteen years old," and two genitally mutilated teenage boys. Following these children were several other Tainos. The Christians captured a few Caribs and—on the order of the Admiral who hoped to help the Tainos to the west as well as assist his Enterprise—destroyed all the dugouts the sailors found.

Carrying away its cargo of Indians rescued from the terror of the roasting spit, the fleet sailed on northward along the range of the Leewards, Columbus naming islands (five of them Mary this or that) as the ships made their way toward La Navidad on Hispaniola and the men left behind ten months earlier. It was a lovely passage through a beautiful seaside realm that was on the verge of witnessing the first unequivocal expressions of conquistadorism.

three

The four days of sailing on the western side of the Leeward Islands marked the end of sweet cruising and largely untroubled explorations. On the morning of the fourteenth of November, the fleet approached an isle Columbus named Santa Cruz (today St. Croix), a beautiful place of cultivated gardens that even Europeans could admire, a land more densely populated than anything they'd yet encountered. The ships moved beyond the barrier reefs at what is now Christiansted Harbor until they reached Salt River Bay where the fleet stopped to take on fresh water. On the very first future territory of the United States Columbus reached, the very first real trouble occurred.

Caribs near the bay fled when the longboats came

ashore, and on a reconnoiter inland, the sailors and men-at-arms found nothing more than a village empty but for a few Taino captives—more children who were taken back to the launches. As the Spaniards started toward the anchored fleet, into view came a canoe bearing seven people, two of them women and one a Taino boy whose castration had not yet healed. The Indians stopped, profoundly startled to discover such an assemblage of huge and strange vessels; as they gawked in disbelief, the Christians rowed toward them to prevent their turning about. Unable to escape, the men and both women took up bows and let loose enough arrows to injure two Spaniards, one of them taking an arrow so powerfully launched it passed through his shield. The longboat rammed the dugout and sent the Indians into the sea, but they swam to a rock to continue fighting until they were overwhelmed and taken aboard the *Maríagalante* for the Admiral's inspection. Peter Martyr, reading or hearing the account of an eyewitness, says of those captured Caribs whose practice was to shave half of their head while leaving the other side in long hair: "They [then] did no more put off their fierceness and cruel countenance than do the lions of Libya when they perceive themselves to be bound in chains. There is no man able to behold them but he shall feel his bowels grate with a certain horror, nature hath endowed them with so terrible, menacing, and cruel aspect."

The flagship surgeon looked at one Carib badly

wounded enough that his intestines were exposed, and pronounced him doomed: The Christians pitched him into the bay, whereupon, holding his innards as best he could, he struck out for shore. The Tainos warned he would report the attack if he survived, so the fellow was pulled from the water and tied hand and foot, and tossed back into the bay. He bobbed to the surface, freed himself from his bonds, and again took off swimming. The sailors then filled him with arrows until he went under.

By that time other Caribs had come to the shore, milling in anger and shouting, their painted bodies and distinctively shaved heads accentuating their ferocity, but their arrows couldn't reach the ships. During the uproar, several desperate Taino captives seized the moment to break loose and swim out to the fleet, but the brutality didn't end with that happy rescue.

One of the most astonishing descriptions in the history of the Spanish conquest of the Americas is a shameless letter home by Michele de Cuneo:

> While I was in the boat I captured a very beautiful Carib woman whom the Lord Admiral gave to me, and with whom, having taken her into my cabin, she being naked according to their custom, I conceived desire to take pleasure. I wanted to put my desire into execution but she did not want it and treated me with her finger nails in such a manner that I wished I had never begun. But seeing that,

(to tell you the end of it all), I took a rope and thrashed her well, for which she raised such unheard of screams that you would not have believed your ears. Finally we came to an agreement in such manner that I can tell you that she seemed to have been brought up in a school of harlots.

People who believe that Divine Hands of Justice mete out rewards and punishments for human actions need look no further than that November day in 1493 on the Island of the Holy Cross for reasons why the fortunes of Columbus almost immediately began to turn. Other people wanting to leave Providence of any kind out of it, can look directly to the Admiral himself for his attitudes and beliefs—religious, political, economic—that were coming to the fore, bringing with them repercussions that would last for generations. Columbus, never adept in accepting his own role in his ultimate fate, apparently saw himself blameless in such actions despite his practice of handing over to his men Indian women.

four

For another few days the easier aspect of the second expedition resumed as the fleet sailed on through more of the Virgin Islands, named by Columbus this time not after the Virgin Mary but for Saint Ursula and the legend, in one version, of her three-year voyage with eleven thousand virgins and the Pope. The Admiral passed westward to the eastern end of Puerto Rico and followed its beautiful southern coast to the end where he stopped for two days to take on fresh water and send an exploring party ashore. Fortunately, on this second territory of the future United States he reached, the natives disappeared, and there were no rapes or killings. Still following the directions of the Taino pilots, he crossed Mona Passage to the eastern tip of Hispaniola—the Dominican Republic today—and entered waters he recognized.

The Basque seaman wounded by the Carib arrow that penetrated his shield died, the first known European casualty of the Columbian expeditions. His shipmates stopped to bury him onshore, and while there, the Admiral released a Taino taken to Spain, probably one of only two to survive long enough to return home. This action, like others before it, was not humanitarian but strategic because Columbus expected the Indian, laden with trade items, to spread the word about the friendliness of the Christians.

As the Admiral sailed west toward La Navidad, everywhere alert for a location to set up a colony nearer the reputed gold mines of Cibao on the interior of Hispaniola, he twice paused to look at possible sites, but what he found was the first indication that colonization might be more difficult than he had represented to the Crown. Sailors exploring along a riverbank came upon a pair of corpses, both bound with cords, the cadavers too

107

decomposed for identification, although a thick beard was still visible on one. The following day, another pair of rotting bodies turned up. Concerned about what the carcasses might portend, Columbus hastened on toward La Navidad, where he arrived just after dusk on the twenty-seventh of November. Flares from the ships received no answer from shore, nor did the discharge of onboard cannons bring a reply. Knowing what silence likely meant, Columbus grew worried.

His hopes rose a little before midnight when a canoe approached the fleet and a couple of Tainos called out for him, although they refused to come aboard *Maria-galante* until torchlight illuminated Columbus. One of the natives was cousin to Guacanagari who was sending his Christian friend more golden masks. The Indians indicated things were well at La Navidad except for sickness and a quarrel or two. In fact, they said, their cacique could not pay a visit because of a wound he suffered in a skirmish protecting the fortress from another chief. Over the next few hours, the Admiral's Taino interpreter, baptized as Diego, managed to draw out more details: The truth was that La Navidad had been destroyed. Columbus was incredulous. How could timid Tainos overcome forty armed Spaniards?

Dawn revealed the fortress was indeed gone, burned to nothing but refuse, and some Tainos standing nearby seemed skittish and hurried away at the approach of the longboats. Guacanagari's cousin returned and, lured by the tinkle of hawk bells, came aboard and disclosed more: All the Europeans had been killed by warriors of a cacique named Caonabo, and Guacanagari's wound that kept him away was a result of trying to defend the garrison. Unsatisfied, Columbus the next day inspected the ruins in hopes of turning up more evidence but found nothing conclusive, although on a walk down the beach to a scattering of moldy huts he found Spanish stockings, a Moorish scarf, and an anchor from *Santa María*. At his return, several Tainos paused in trading trinkets to show him eleven decomposing bodies, several weeks dead.

Over the next couple of days, Columbus received invitations to call upon Guacanagari; he accepted and went forth with a procession of some one hundred armed men marching along to the beat of drummers. The cacique lay in a hammock and appeared much troubled by his injured thigh wrapped in a dressing. He said there had been trouble among the Spaniards that spread inland until it reached Caonabo who refused to brook it and moved against La Navidad in the night and torched it. Columbus asked his surgeon to treat Guacanagari's wound. When the physician unwrapped the thigh, he saw a leg without blemish. Still weighing things, the Admiral invited the pretending invalid to supper that evening aboard the *Mariagalante,* and Guacanagari quickly found himself recovered enough to join in.

After the meal, Columbus gathered his staff to decide what action to take. A reverend father sent to minister to the Indians argued that Guacanagari was lying and should be executed immediately to establish royal and ecclesiastical authority. Columbus, in one of his astute moments, trusted his friendship with the cacique and also considered how the Spanish were outnumbered; perhaps too he realized he'd misreckoned the docility of the Indians. He decided to wait for better evidence. The fleet sailed back eastward along the north shore of Haiti in search of a safer and more convenient site for a settlement.

What actually happened at the first Spanish attempt to establish a presence in the Americas came to light during the next few years as invaders and aboriginals learned each other's language. That story should surprise no one. Soon after *Niña* departed in January 1493, the men of La Navidad began bickering over—what else?—gold and women. The Christians robbed Tainos of one and stole away the other, until each Spaniard possessed four or five females. The sailors fell into competing gangs and began killing each other as they made forays inland to answer their lusts, before the marauders troubled Caonabo, a leader reportedly with some Carib ancestry. His warriors hunted down the gangs and picked off the sailors till there weren't enough to defend the fortress, enabling Caonabo to take it in the night and wipe out the remaining Europeans. Guacanagari, who remained loyal to Columbus to the end, likely did try to defend La Navidad, and the sham wound was probably only an attempt to cover embarrassment over failure to help his friend.

The hubris of the foreigners in their contempt for their hosts and the unmitigated barbarism of their lusts undid them. As apparent even then as the short history of La Navidad was—and would become more so later— Columbus and all of Europe learned little from it. What might have been the nativity of a great and peaceful cultural exchange was instead the first chapter in the story of the shame of Christopher Columbus.

five

Struggling against unfavorable winds, the fleet worked hard for more than three weeks to gain only thirty-two miles. Partly out of necessity created by the bad sailing weather, but even more because of dying animals, exhausted men, and the necessity of finding gold to prove the worth of the Second Voyage, the ships somewhat prematurely dropped anchor on the northern coast of the Dominican Republic on the second day of 1494. The Admiral selected a better site than La Navidad but one still less than ideal. He named it La Isabela after his queen and hoped it would last centuries. A couple of hundred huts went up, but that progress did not stem the grumblings and mutinous schemes of some alleged colonists more devoted to making fast wealth than to laying the foundation for a new empire.

The Admiral sent two small reconnaissance expeditions into the Cibao, the inland mountain valleys of the island, to hunt for gold, and both groups returned with nuggets and dust, but only what the Tainos had given them. With that lucre as evidence of more to come and also needing resupply, Columbus dispatched twelve of his seventeen ships for Cadiz on the second of February. Aboard were some two dozen Indians destined for the slave market in Seville. When the fleet reached Spain about a month later, the gold and the Admiral's report went off to the King and Queen who were pleased enough to order fulfilled all his requests for more men and matériel. To the Crown, its first colonial adventure looked promising.

But at fortress La Isabela several hundred men lay sick, complaints were increasing, and plots hatching. To help quell the discontent, on the first of March Columbus led a large contingent of armed men and skilled workmen into the Cibao to build an inland post, the first of its kind in the New World. That military column was the precursor to those the infamous conquistadors—Pizzaro, De Soto, Cortés, Coronado, and others—would soon employ in ransacking more than half of the Americas from Texas to Tierra del Fuego. As the column marched through the interior one witness described as a paradise, the soldiers accepted what the generous Tainos offered, and when there was no offer, the Christians took what they wanted except in a cluster of houses the natives closed up as best they could before fleeing; aware of the usefulness of cooperative neighbors, Columbus ordered those places left alone.

He found a site to his liking not far from the present city of Santiago, and there his men set to work on constructing the fort of Santo Tomás, perhaps a jibe at those who had doubted the success of his Enterprise. The location proved to be a good one, for in the Greater Antilles the Cordillera Central is the heart of gold country. The Indians continued giving and trading gold—nuggets, dust, artifacts—and the major problem of collection became not one of mining but rather of trying to prevent private dealings. Any Christian caught so engaged was whipped or, in some cases, had his nose or ears slit.

After seventeen days, Columbus left behind enough men to complete and garrison Santo Tomás, and he returned to La Isabela. Crops were coming up in the rich soil, but that wasn't the yield the men wanted most zealously; Cuneo writes, "Out of covetousness for that gold, we all kept strong and lusty." True for some like himself, but for others life in La Isabela was an early burial. Yet relations between Spaniards and Tainos remained tolerable. If the resupply ships could arrive soon enough, the Admiral's plans for a trading colony might work.

On the ninth of April he sent some of the troublemakers—accompanied by good workers—to relieve those at Santo Tomás while other men commenced another reconnaissance. The expedition leader, Alonso de Hojeda (who would later make a name for himself as an explorer of the southern Caribbean), came upon a few Tainos who had made off with several pieces of Spanish clothing when the Indians were helping the foreigners across a river. Hojeda caught the pilferers, cut the ears off one, then captured their cacique and two of his relatives who had received the garments; he put them in chains and marched them to La Isabela. Las Casas says of the incident, "This was the first injustice, with vain and erroneous pretension of doing justice, that was committed in these Indies against the Indians, and the beginning of the shedding of blood which has since flowed so copiously."

The Admiral looked at the captives and ordered them beheaded. Months of Taino generosity to him seemed to count for nothing until another cacique came forward to plead for the Indians' lives. Columbus rescinded his edict, but by then the Tainos saw clearly what the Christians were capable of.

six

Columbus had realized by then that Hispaniola was neither the island of Cipango nor some portion of mainland Asia, but he still believed the Asian coast lay nearby, and he continued determined to find the Grand Khan. On April twenty-fourth, he again went to sea to explore, the thing he did far better than found colonies. For this coasting, he left *Maríagalante* behind at La Isabela and made the smaller but redoubtable *Niña* once more his flagship; in her company were two other caravels, the trio carrying a total complement of about sixty trusted mariners. Their first destination was Cuba.

One account of this portion of the Second Voyage comes from Andrés Bernáldez who housed Columbus for more than a month when the Admiral returned to Spain and recounted his adventures. We may assume that Bernáldez expresses geographical conceptions of the great navigator himself in a sentence like this: "If one should set forth by land from Cape St. Vincent [in western Portugal] he could always go eastward without crossing any part of the Ocean Sea until he arrived at Cape Alfa et Omega [in eastern Cuba]." This idea is, of course, correct but for two errors: the comparatively minor one involving two hundred miles of the Yucatán Channel in the Caribbean Sea; but the second mistake is of another order—the Pacific Ocean.

By the end of April, the Admiral was following along the southern coast of Cuba where he and his men would become the first Europeans to see the great bay at Guantánamo. There the ships stopped to reconnoiter. Columbus found neither the Grand Khan nor one of his marvelous cities, but only a campfire attended by a barkless dog. Roasting on spits were a pair of iguanas the Europeans deemed too revolting even to taste, although they did help themselves to a slew of smoked fish. Several natives reappeared on a nearby hill and gave friendly signals. Through Taino interpreter Diego, Columbus learned the Indians were preparing food for a feast they would carry to their cacique, but they were happy to share the fish—and even happier when the Spaniards showed no appetite for difficult-to-catch lizards.

All along the coast, Cubans came to shore or paddled out to offer casava bread and gourds of fresh water, often addressing the mariners as people from the sky, never mind Diego's explanation that the bearded ones came merely from across the sea. Over this coastal run, incidentally, Columbus sailed right through the place where, 404 years later, the Hispanic hegemony in the Americas he initiated would come to a close with the surrender to the U.S. Navy of a Spanish cruiser named *Cristóbal Colón*.

The Indians of that area told Columbus he could find gold on an island not far south, one the Admiral named Santiago and the Indians called Jamaica. That was the next destination. Jamaican Tainos, a less tractable group than others the Christians encountered, built huge dugout canoes, some of them longer than a Spanish caravel, and on the bows and sterns they carved and painted elaborate decorations, and the warriors were not afraid of taking the craft into battle. On his first approach to the island west of present St. Ann's Bay, Columbus chanced upon about seventy canoes full of yelling and threatening natives swiftly heading toward the little fleet. He called for a blank fusillade of cannon fire that convinced the Indians to turn back to shore, and then he sent interpreter Diego off in a longboat to explain things. Soon a

Jamaican canoe approached *Niña* and received the usual trade gewgaws. The next day, fifteen miles farther west, another bellicose reception happened, but in this one Columbus decided to ignore diplomacy and answered hurled spears and stones with arrows from his crossbowmen who killed, says Cuneo, "sixteen or eighteen of them," and the cannoneers got half a dozen more. When the Christians reached shore, they unleashed a large war dog that Bernáldez says "bit and did them great hurt, for a dog is worth ten men against Indians." Canine attack against the Indians is another Columbian first of the baneful kind.

The caravels needed fresh water and wood, and their hulls required recaulking, so the fleet had to stay in that seemingly inhospitable territory four days, but the Admiral's diplomacy by death worked: The next morning the Jamaicans brought to him expiatory gifts of fish and fruit and received beads and hawk bells. Among the offerings there was no gold in any form, and that absence proved a beneficence for those Tainos: The Christians returned to Cuba.

From the middle of May until mid-June, the caravels sailed closely along the southern Cuban shore and in several places met with warm receptions but ones also lacking gold. At the first of them, Columbus was amazed to find Indians who had heard of him from his Cuban explorations on the initial voyage. Farther west, he came upon an elderly man whose language Diego couldn't interpret, but neither he nor Columbus had any idea they were looking at one of the last Siboneys, the indigenous people whom the Tainos had largely dispossessed. Of more interest was the report from a Spanish hunter who said he had been chased by some natives whose leader was a man in a long white tunic. That person, so concluded Columbus, had to be a descendant of the legendary priest-king, Prester John, a figure to help confirm the fleet was indeed sailing in Asian waters and to give evidence more convincing than Mandeville-like Indian stories there about people with tails. Further, Columbus had heard Tainos refer to western Cuba as Magon, which sounded, he thought, like a variation on the name for the southern Chinese province of Mangi. Things were fitting together so well for him—in spite of one stubborn Indian who adamantly held to his statement that Cuba was an island.

It is surprising that throughout his explorations, the Taino pilots never indicated to Columbus that a second ocean and two continents and many marvelous cities lay not far away. Since the Tainos seemed willing to disclose their geographical knowledge, we must wonder whether they were aware of the great Indian civilizations just beyond the Caribbean they knew so well.

Trying to stay close to shore, Columbus entered west of the Bay of Pigs, an area that was and is a vast shallow embayment full of small islands and cays. Progress became treacherous and tiring. In a place or two, the seamen even had to resort to kedging the ships through, that is, using a longboat to carry ahead an anchor, dropping it, then winching the ship forward along the anchor cable, hull dragging all the way. Such farmerlike labor wears out a mariner's wish to continue. When the fleet was within fifty miles of the most westward tip of Cuba, Columbus considered his men's morale and the hulls damaged from dragging through shoals, and he decided to turn back east. After all, no southern European had ever heard of any island as long as Cuba, especially one lying latitudinally. All the evidence suggested to him he was skirting a peninsula, and that information was apparently good enough just then. Perhaps to cover his decision to return without incontrovertible proof of the Asian mainland, Columbus sent his secretary onto each vessel to take depositions declaring that Cuba was the Asian continent; any man who later might gainsay his declaration would receive a hefty fine and have his tongue cut out, or, in the case of ships' boys, the threat was a hundred lashes on a naked back. Such inquisitional methods to enforce preconceived doctrine helped keep forever the truth of his discoveries from Columbus.

Had the fleet sailed on over those last few westerly miles, the insularity of Cuba would have stood revealed and the Admiral might even have been able to continue only another two hundred miles to find a true mainland peninsula—the Yucatán—where there were indeed precious stones and gold and fabulous cities; although in ruin, they might have encouraged him to continue westward to find what he so deeply dreamed of reaching. Perhaps the Gulf Stream would have pulled him northward to the not-far-distant Florida Keys. Beyond these things, he at least could have learned the impossibility of his wish to return to Spain by sailing on west. But his decision to wheel around and enter the extensive and treacherous shoals of the Gulf of Batabanó, while an execution of brilliant seamanship in getting all his ships safely through, cost him the chance to discover where lay the great wealth and geographical knowledge that were the real goals of his explorations.

seven

The return to La Isabela, beginning on June thirteenth, took three and half months, with some of the time given to exploration, yet much of it also went simply to struggling through more shoals that contentious winds forced the fleet into. During one onerous day, *Niña* went aground and sustained damage, but not enough to stop her. When the blowing finally allowed the ships to escape the shallows, thunder squalls struck and forced Columbus into layovers that threatened to exhaust provisions. Had it not been for the generosity—again— of the Tainos on several islands, the lot of the Christians would have been severe indeed. During these struggles, no one gave greater effort than the Admiral, but his long and unremitting efforts weakened his strong constitution.

There were moments of relief, the kind of events mariners require in order to continue in other travails. On one day the caravels came upon a vast swarming of sea turtles, so many that, writes Bernáldez, "it seemed as if the ships would run aground on them, and their shells actually clattered" against the hulls. In another place, seamen looked into the clear water and discovered conchs so big it required both hands to pick them up for cooking. Later, when the fleet came upon a bed of huge oysters, sailors heaped the longboats full and eagerly opened shells in search of fat pearls, but all the men got was a feast.

With the trade winds against him, Columbus decided in July to explore more of the Jamaican coast despite the hostility of his first two encounters there; along the south shore, he found the Tainos more amicable than those on the north. At one anchorage, a cacique with his wife, two teenage daughters, two sons, five brothers, and an accompanying entourage—all quite naked but for some elaborately feathered headgear—paddled out to *Niña* to request passage for all of them to the majestic realm of the Admiral's Sovereigns, so grandiloquently and repeatedly interpreted by Diego. Realizing the impracticality of getting such a resplendent display of Taino rank back to Castile, Columbus said no to their wish and saved the disappointed innocents from premature ends.

By late August the flotilla had reached the south side of Hispaniola where it received more crucial help from the Tainos. As the caravels came around the eastern end of the island, instead of continuing on back to La Isabela, the Admiral uncharacteristically changed his plans and decided to go again into Carib country either to *destroy* their canoes—and so protect the Tainos while perhaps taking some slaves—or to *discover* more about them. Because of a question in transcription of a word, his intent is not clear on this important idea, but the question is moot: For the first time, a fever felled him and left him thrashing between delirium and unconsciousness. His staff gathered and decided to return at once to La Isabela.

On September twenty-ninth, the much beaten trio of caravels reached the settlement and dropped anchors among a welcome sight—three relief ships recently come from Spain. Among the men arriving was Bartholomew Columbus who had missed Christopher's second departure as he did the first. The seamen carried the sick Admiral to his brothers with his news of the western lands and not finding a smidgen of gold nor a single pearl anywhere. As Columbus slowly recovered, he finally had at his side a man of intelligence, courage, strength, and unbreakable loyalty. Bartholomew, who had helped devise the Enterprise of the Indies years before, was now present to serve as advisor and executive officer, roles the cloistral Diego never could adequately fulfill.

eight

Columbus had left brother Diego to establish the colony, but he was not the man for such an undertaking, and he proved incapable of preventing the thug factions among the Christians from running amok. Before departing on the Cuban-Jamaican expedition, the Admiral gave instructions not to wrong the Tainos—except to punish theft by cutting off noses and ears—while exploring the island and discovering its resources. During his absence, one of his lieutenants, Pedro Margarit, as villainous a man as any there, set off into the hinterland with almost four hundred armed men under the pretext of reconnaissance. Carrying no food and far too little trading truck to barter for provisions, they took to stealing from the Tainos who traditionally relied upon the abundance and ever-productive climate of their land for continued sustenance. Their communal existence did not require large stores of foodstuff; they shared what they had, but they didn't have much. Las Casas, even if somewhat overstating, mentions another element of the problem: "One Spaniard ate more in a day than a whole family of natives would consume in a month."

Margarit and his hoodlums roamed the country, exhausting the food for everyone and everywhere exacting gold from the Tainos through intimidation and beatings; the Christians raped women and kidnapped children into slavery. In Pedro Margarit, a name deserving lasting opprobrium, the great conquistadorial nightmare found its first full expression in the New World.

When Diego Columbus ordered Margarit to cease the brutality, the brigand went into a fury at the rebuke and linked up his thugs with some malcontents—including the Most Reverend Father Bernal Buil who was supposed to be converting the Indians—and forcibly took command of the relief ships and sailed them off for Spain. Many of the remaining Christians formed into new gangs and ranged over Hispaniola in a continuing pillage of the island and rape of its residents, some of whom began, however ineffectually, to fight back.

Columbus attempted to restore order in a way most ugly. Again utterly ignoring the many acts of generosity and benignity Tainos had repeatedly rendered to keep him and his men alive, he turned on his hosts and sent troops out to hunt them down with superior weapons and war dogs. In no time, the pitiless Europeans brought back to La Isabela more than fifteen hundred stunned and terrorized Tainos. About a third of them, selected as the best specimens of men and women, were herded onto four resupply vessels and locked in belowdecks for shipment to the Seville slave market. Of the rest, Columbus decreed, any Christian could take as many as he wanted. He then allowed four hundred Tainos remaining to run for the hills.

Nearly all the gold the Spaniards extorted they hid away in private stashes, leaving Columbus with a primary cargo of human flesh to help cover the cost of his expeditions. His cold-blooded decision was not, however, brought on simply by a need for expediency. It was worse than that: He was now enacting a plan he'd hatched on the First Voyage of forcing natives into labor to enrich Spanish coffers, a system that would take the name *encomienda*. Now, two years later, he was contriving a slave trade in Caribs, despite messages from Ferdinand and Isabella ordering a delay in such traffic until there was discussion. Nevertheless, when the second group of four resupply ships sailed back to Cadiz in February 1495, aboard them were half a thousand Tainos confined belowdecks in incredibly cramped and fetid misery. The flotilla leader, not knowing how to use the westerlies, spent three weeks fumbling about in the eastern islands before finally moving north where he found winds to push the fleet on to Spain. Conditions in the holds of the ships created a hell the Tainos could never have imagined: tainted food, contaminated water, foul air, decks poisonous with human wastes, people ill, people dying, all of them battered by the sea. And ahead for those who could endure was slavery, a condition none of them long survived. All of this incalculable suffering was orchestrated by an intelligent man who believed his work was directed by the hand of his God.

For the Tainos still in Hispaniola, things were scarcely better. Toward the end of March 1495, Columbus led a force of more than two hundred men and twenty war dogs into the upcountry to hunt down the most effective leader of Taino opposition, the cacique Guatiguana. It didn't take long to find him, and when the Spaniards did, their horses, dogs, and weapons quickly overcame him and his warriors; those who survived were taken for the slave market. Guacanagari, always loyal to Columbus, assisted in defeating his fellow Tainos.

Still free was Caonabo, the destroyer of La Navidad after Christians depredated his people. The Admiral sent out Alonso de Hojeda, the ruthless little man, to seize the cacique by force or fraud. The diminutive Christian invited Caonabo to La Isabela to make peace, promising he could have the much-beloved church bell. When groups from both sides met some distance from the fortress, Hojeda showed the cacique a pair of polished bracelets and matching set of anklets and told him the Spanish King wore such things while riding his horse in great festivals. Would he like to put them on in kingly fashion and ride royally into La Isabela? Caonabo climbed onto the horse behind Hojeda and allowed himself to be tied to the captain to keep the cacique from falling off so strange and fearful a beast. Then the Spaniards honored him by slipping on him the bracelets and anklets; seated proudly, Caonabo looked at his countrymen as the Christian spurred the horse. It was not until the Taino chief was imprisoned in La Isabela that he learned about handcuffs and leg chains.

His brother-in-law offered the strongest resistance, but

he too fell, and with his demise the Tainos were effectively vanquished, and Columbus was able to make a triumphal march into the countryside. His son Ferdinand wrote that not long afterward, a Christian could travel alone and without fear throughout Hispaniola and take what food and women he liked. The natives would even carry him on their backs across a stream.

nine

With Hispaniola in submission, Columbus and his brothers took their next steps toward economic colonization by building three more inland forts that served as posts for soldiers to patrol the country and force Tainos into collecting gold for Spain. Every three months each native older than thirteen had to find and turn over enough gold dust to fill a hawk bell. Those who failed had a hand cut off. People living beyond the gold region paid their tribute with twenty-five pounds of spun or woven cotton. To prove payment of the levy, an Indian received a marked token to wear around the neck.

Gold ornaments and nuggets that had taken the Tainos generations to accumulate through a slow gathering of bits of the metal, those very things they at first so freely gave or traded for tiny bells and cheap beads, were now gone, and the tiresome, unremitting, and often unproductive labor of sifting gold dust from sand was their only source. Columbus turned them into virtual slave laborers facing impossible extortion. Finally recognizing his plan was hardly workable, he cut the tribute by half, and still the Tainos could not meet his requirement. Las Casas says:

> [The Indians fell] into the most wretched way of living; some took refuge in the mountains whilst others, since the violence and provocation and injuries on the part of the Christians never ceased, killed some Christian for special damages and tortures that they suffered. Then straightaway against them was taken the vengeance which the Christians called punishment; not only the murderers, but as many as might be in that village or region were punished with execution and torture.

Those who fled were hunted down and torn apart by dogs, and some people who could escape concocted a deadly drink from casava, once the source for their staff of life. Samuel Eliot Morison wrote in 1942:

> The policy and acts of Columbus for which he alone was responsible began the depopulation of the terrestrial paradise that was Hispaniola in 1492. Of the original natives, estimated by a modern ethnologist at 300,000 in number, one third were killed off between 1494 and 1496. By 1508 an enumeration showed only 60,000 alive. Four years later that

number was reduced by two thirds; and in 1548 Oviedo doubted whether 500 Indians remained.

Whether any Tainos remain today depends on a definition of the name.

In October 1495, four more resupply ships arrived at La Isabela. In command was Juan Aguado who had come out with Columbus on the Second Voyage but returned to Spain with the first shipment of slaves. Although he was nothing more than a chamberlain sent by the Crown to look into conditions on the island, he gave himself authority as if he were viceroy of Hispaniola and ordered his minions to document the discontent of the Spanish looters; scribes found almost everyone wanting to leave a paradise they had turned into a hell. Before his departure, Michele de Cuneo explained part of the cause: "Although the soil is very black and good [the men here] have not yet found the way nor the time to sow; the reason is that nobody wants to live in these countries." That began to change soon after, but for the Tainos, it came too late.

Knowing he would need to return to Spain to stand before the King and Queen and give answer to charges by Margarit and Buil (not about brutality but about alleged greed) and eventually address ones by Aguado harder to deny, Columbus prepared to leave, but a hurricane swept over La Isabela and shattered three ships; once again, only *Niña* withstood the elements. The Admiral told his shipwrights to salvage the wrecks and assemble a caravel that could accompany *Niña* home. This first ship built in the Americas, formally known as *Santa Cruz,* was to the seamen *India,* the place Columbus told them they were. When she was finished around March 1496, he boarded *Niña* and, in the company of the cobbled-together *India,* set off on his second return voyage.

His final instruction to Bartholomew was to build a new town in a better location than La Isabela. After several searches, the conquerors decided on a place across the island on the south coast, one close to a source of gold. Today, Santo Domingo, the capital of the Dominican Republic, continues as the oldest surviving, European-built city in the Western Hemisphere. As for La Isabela, that place of heinous history, it soon fell to ruin, and even before the last Taino disappeared, the iniquity executed there haunted it. Morison reports:

> Terrible cries were heard by hunters who approached the place, and once in a deserted street a benighted traveler met two *caballeros* booted and spurred, with swords by their sides, and cloaked like courtiers of olden time, who on being saluted returned his courtesy with low and sweeping bows; but their heads came off with their hats, and their bodies disappeared. So men avoided the site of Isabela, and today [1942] it is a pasture by the sea with only a few stones above the ground to show that once it was the capital city of the Spanish Indies.

ten

When *Niña* and *India* got under way on the morning of March 10, 1496, Columbus had been in the Caribbean for nearly two and a half years. During that time he had visited all the large islands, and although he didn't know it—the usual Columbian situation—his Taino guides had assisted his own expert navigational powers to allow him to cover most of the Y-shaped Antillean archipelago. On the sea, he had performed well, but ashore he'd shown himself to be a colonizer capable of executing a plan only through brute intimidation.

The two caravels were dangerously overcrowded with 225 Spaniards desperately wanting to go home and thirty Indians wishing to stay home; one of them was probably Caonabo who did not survive the crossing. Columbian luck continued slipping, a pattern that would remain almost unbroken for much of the rest of his life. Aware that the ships were carrying four to five times more people than their usual complement, he chose a direct line for home but one that kept him from finding favoring westerlies and forced him to buck less coopera-tive winds all the way, thereby turning a potential four-week voyage into one of three months. Thirty days after leaving La Isabela, the scrubby flotilla was still only in the eastern Antilles, and sweet water and food were already running low.

On the tenth of April, the ships stopped in Guadeloupe

near the anchorage of almost three years earlier when his scouting party got lost for several days among the Caribs. On this layover, seamen took longboats toward a host of women who suddenly charged and let fly a volley of arrows that the sailors managed to duck. Columbus dispatched some of his Taino women captives to go ashore and explain that he wanted only water and casava bread. The Caribs said their men were in the north of the island and might help, but once there, the Spaniards rowed into another assault of arrows, perhaps an ambush, and again the cannons had to open the way. The Christians looted huts but came away without any bread or other food, so a squad of armed men went in pursuit of Indians and managed to nab three boys and ten women who served as hostages to force a trade of casava; over the next nine days, the captive Tainos managed to turn the roots into what Columbus hoped was enough bread to see them across the ocean. Griddle cakes made from the plant could retain flavor and freshness well, and in subsequent years they became something of a staple aboard Hispanic ships.

On the twentieth of April, the little fleet went off into the area of the Atlantic unfriendly in winds and currents to any ship sailing east. By the end of a month, food was again running so low that Columbus put everyone on short rations of six ounces of bread and a cup of water, the Indians probably receiving even less. The Christians discussed whether eating Caribs or merely throwing them overboard to save their rations would best serve. Believing the flesh of flesh-eaters would make them ill complicated the argument. Ferdinand Columbus writes that his father managed to delay this deadly decision just long enough until the coast of Portugal appeared on the horizon. Once again, the Admiral, despite the poor route he'd chosen, was able to dead-reckon a course that brought the flotilla within about thirty-five miles of the cape he was trying to reach, another stunning navigational feat.

On the eleventh of June, 1496, the two weather-wasted ships, one with uncounted leagues under her hull and the other pieced together from salvage, entered Cadiz harbor. Their flags and banners could not hide the debilitated Europeans and ill and dying Indians from sailors aboard two caravels ready to depart for Hispaniola. That woeful sight must have been demoralizing, and possibly enlightening, to men eager for the New World.

Once disembarked from *Niña*, Columbus did a peculiar and revealing thing, for it was then he took up wearing while in Spain the simple brown robe of a Franciscan friar. Neither he nor anyone else elucidated his reason, but it might have been his wish to atone for pride that seemed to be bringing troubles upon him, or perhaps it was a desire to deflect attention from himself at a time enemies were succeeding in denigrating him and his enterprise. Europe was no longer agog over his explorations. To cite one instance, a metallurgist who had shipped out on the Second Voyage but whom Columbus had sent home for insubordination was claiming Caribbean gold was nothing but an alloy, perhaps a lie useful to escape paying the mandated share due the Crown and the Admiral. Whatever his motivation for Franciscan garmenture, Columbus was becoming ever more comfortable in the peaceful and restorative company of men in monastic orders.

The Third Voyage

one

Columbus went from Cadiz to near Seville, not a long journey, to stay with Andrés Bernáldez, chaplain to the archbishop there. The inquisitive priest gave Columbus a place to recuperate while the Admiral told about the realms he had visited and the ways of the Indians, and it was with Bernáldez that he left his logbooks of the Second Voyage, ones now vanished. After some time, the Crown invited him to visit and present his report.

During that summer of 1496, Columbus saw that the bright and novel promise of his Enterprise had diminished, so he assembled a cortege to accompany him north for his appearance at court and to reinspire along the way citizens dubious about the worth of his findings west of the Ocean Sea. Among the retinue led by men carrying cages of garrulous and gaudy parrots were Caonabo's two relatives who, upon nearing a village, would don the

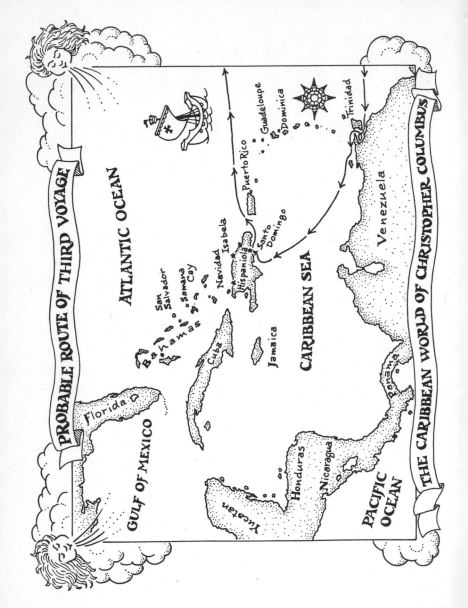

PROBABLE ROUTE OF THIRD VOYAGE

THE CARIBBEAN WORLD OF CHRISTOPHER COLUMBUS

ATLANTIC OCEAN

Guadeloupe

Dominica

Trinidad

Puerto Rico

Venezuela

San Salvador

Senana Cay

Navidad

Isabela

Santo Domingo

Hispaniola

Bahamas

Cuba

Jamaica

CARIBBEAN SEA

Florida

GULF OF MEXICO

Panama

Honduras

Nicaragua

Yucatan

PACIFIC OCEAN

136

best golden ornaments and feathered headdresses. This circus parade was a strategy to further the Admiral's wish for another expedition.

Ferdinand and Isabella received him well, an encouraging response perhaps assisted by his sons who were now pages to Infante Don Juan. The pageantry of his calvacade and the display of golden artifacts, sacks of gold dust, and some nuggets the size of peanuts undoubtedly also aided his reception and helped negate accusations from some of the Hispaniola brigands like Pedro Margarit and the more justified charges of misgovernance by Father Buil who was never a supporter of Columbus.

The Sovereigns assented to a Third Voyage of discovery, motivated now by the additional wish to prevent or delay a Caribbean incursion by a rival like Portugal, which was equipping an imminent expedition for India under the leadership of a mariner named Vasco da Gama. But Ferdinand and Isabella and their treasury were deeply involved in the continental politics of consolidating their power through alliances and royal marriages, and plans for part three of the Enterprise of the Indies proceeded slowly.

Among their orders for the endeavor was one offering pardon to anyone imprisoned for minor crimes (pickpockets not counterfeiters, prostitutes not sodomites, debtors not heretics), although there may have been several exculpated murderers; in exchange for a year or two on Hispaniola, an inmate could gain amnesty in a place more free if less secure than a cell. The Crown was not turning the island into a prison colony but merely trying to reduce the cost of the Third Voyage, the first to include a few women.

Months of waiting and struggling fatigued Columbus who wrote Bartholomew in the Caribbean that he had not seen before such obstacles nor suffered such anxieties of preparation. Poor health apparently made things additionally difficult. He even took his fists to a ship chandler after several broken promises and delays. Finally, at the end of May 1498, two years after his second return to Spain, the Admiral had five caravels (with a pair sent ahead) and a flagship similar to his first *Santa María* ready to sail from Seville down the Guadalquivir River and across the Atlantic, in quest of a southern continent suspected by only a few Europeans, one of whom was the late King of Portugal, John II, who presumed it to sprawl out somewhere below the equator.

two

Ancient geographers theorized that lands lying near the same latitude held similar resources and that gold regions occurred in zones close to the equator. Believing the notion at least possible, Columbus planned on his Third Voyage to sail a more southerly course aligned with the gold fields of Sierra Leone. Such a route would further his primary goal of searching out a possible equatorial continent, as well as revealing what islands, perhaps gold-bearing ones, might lie south of the Lesser Antilles.

Watchful this time for ships of France, now the enemy of Spain, Columbus sailed southwest with stops at Madeira, the Canaries, and the Cape Verde Islands before taking up a westward heading that carried the fleet smack into the windless Doldrums. For eight days the ships drifted with little more than currents to keep them slowly moving. The delay in the July heat caused provisions to spoil and some wine casks to break open, perhaps from secondary fermentation.

Finally, on July twenty-second the trade winds, which rarely reach that region in midsummer, rose to fill the sails, the first luck to touch the Admiral in some time. Spirits of everyone lifted as the flotilla again moved expeditiously along, but Columbus carried a new concern. Las Casas writes:

[The Admiral] saw that his signal services were held of slight value, and that suddenly the reputation that these Indies at first had enjoyed was sinking and declining by reason of those who had the ear of the Sovereigns, so that day by day he feared greater disfavors, and that the Sovereigns might abandon the enterprise altogether, and that he might thus see his labor and travail go for naught, and he in the end die in poverty.

Although Columbus wasn't yet aware of it, while he struggled in the Doldrums, Vasco da Gama was opening an eastern sea route to the true East Indies.

The Admiral's worry, however, did not impair his seamanship. In the Canaries he sent the three supply ships off separately on a fairly direct course for Hispaniola, but even with sailing directions, the three captains and their pilots still got lost in the southern Antilles and would reach the new port of Santo Domingo on Hispaniola days after Columbus, despite the Admiral's stopping to explore along the coast of Venezuela.

By midday on July thirty-first, a servant, Alonso Pérez, climbed to the crow's nest of the flagship and caught sight of a broken horizon. Earlier on that Third Voyage, the Admiral may have decided to name his first landfall La Isla de la Trinidad, The Isle of the Trinity, and as if to prove to his crew the hand of his Providence was again directing, a jagged silhouette of three peaks rose before them. Or, the triad of hills may have suggested the island name; either way, to him they were a divine sign. Samuel Eliot Morison, who navigated those waters, thought "Columbus's belief in a miracle on this occasion was well justified, for if Alonso Pérez had not happened to go aloft at noon, Trinidad would have been missed."

As he coasted along the south shore of Trinidad, the Admiral searched for fresh water and found it at the best source anywhere near. Further luck—or providence. The sailors rolled onto shore, all of them enlivened to have more than a small wooden deck to walk on, relieved by streams to lave away the salt and grime of the voyage, refreshed with unlimited drafts of cool water after weeks of rationed stale water. When the ships were again under way, Columbus at long last laid eyes on a true mainland, the first *certain* sighting of South America by a European. The date was August 1, 1498. What he saw was a tongue of land thrusting out from the delta of the Orinoco River in eastern Venezuela, but he took the spit for an island and didn't bother to visit. He called it Holy Isle—today Punta Bombeador.

The next morning the fleet anchored again on the south shore of Trinidad to give the men another liberty, with the expectation they might find a warm reception from whomever lived there, perhaps people of the Grand Khan, but events turned out otherwise when a large dugout with a couple of dozen young men came cautiously toward the ships. To the Admiral's disappointment, they were not lushly accoutered Asians but Indians wearing only breechcloths and bandanas and looking like the people of the northern islands. Nevertheless, he wanted to meet them, so he ordered chamber pots and shiny things brought to the rails and banged and flashed before the canoes. The Indians watched impassively. He called upon his fife-and-drum player to strike up a tune to accompany a few prancing sailors. To that vigorous display, the natives, perhaps construing it as a war dance, responded with a flight of arrows. Then, inexplicably, they paddled close enough for the intrepid pilot of a caravel to jump into a canoe and offer a handful of trinkets that held the natives' interest for a while, but they were soon gone and didn't return.

Forty-eight hours later the fleet rounded the western tip of Trinidad and sailed into what is today the Gulf of Paría. The ships had hardly taken up a northerly bearing when Columbus heard a fearsome roaring from behind. He turned to see a rogue wave—possibly created by volcanic activity or a tectonic shift—a wall of water as high as the ships and approaching faster than they could escape. The Admiral later said he could feel the fear the thing created in him long after it reached the fleet and lifted the vessels, hoisting them higher than anything he'd ever experienced and then dropping them into its huge trough. But it didn't top the ships. Once behind it, the flotilla hastened for the gulf to escape the constricted passage they had just sailed through, which Columbus named Mouth of the Serpent. He hoped that northward would lie an exit to open sea, and there *was* one there— an intimidating strait of tidal rips. He turned west to sail along the Paría Peninsula, the entire way believing it also an island.

Near the southeastern end of it, on the fifth of August, the fleet dropped anchor in order to send a boat ashore and claim a place the Admiral called Isla de Gracia. This topographic error prevented him from becoming the first European to set foot on the South American continent;

after all, he didn't need to go ashore on every island he came upon! When the landing party turned up no natives to witness the claim, the fleet moved on west a few miles, and the next day stopped again for a formal taking-possession ceremony, but by then Columbus was suffering from a debilitating inflammation of his eyes, caused, he said, by lack of sleep, but probably an infection. He remained aboard the flagship and sent one of the caravel captains to perform the ceremony, however unwittingly, of planting the flag of Spain in the soil of the fourth-largest continent on earth. Columbus, the adroit navigator who could find his way anywhere, was also adept at missing historic opportunities. That one would not be his last.

Of greater interest to him just then were the dozens of canoes that approached the fleet, each dugout conveying natives offering food and drink—calabashes of alcoholic chicha—and wearing large neck ornaments of golden disks with mirror finishes made from an alloy of gold, silver, and copper, the latter a rare metal for those Indians and a valuable item they identified by sniffing. For a piece of copper, they would trade objects ninety percent gold.

Those people were not Tainos, and no one understood them except by signs, so Columbus resorted to his proven practice of nabbing a few. About this tactic, Las Casas says:

It appears that the Admiral did this unscrupulously, as did he many other times on his First Voyage, it not appearing to him that it was an offense to God and his neighbor, to take free men against their will, separating fathers from sons and wives from husbands . . . a mortal sin of which the Admiral was the efficient cause; and there was the further circumstance that they came out to the ships under tacit security and promised faith which should have been kept.

The fleet sailed on westward, anchoring in another place where the native neckwear was golden ornaments the size of horseshoes and, on women, necklaces of seeds set off by pearls. Could all this be some of the bejeweled wealth of Asia that Marco Polo wrote about? Columbus found further reinforcement just down the coast along a shoreline of mangroves with roots wrapped in small oysters, each open to capture dewdrops that beget pearls—or so said Pliny, another of the Admiral's revered sources. Perhaps he could not find the Grand Khan, but he could believe some of the riches of the Orient were at last coming to light. Let naysayers in Spain grumble on, for now more than ever he was able to envision the wealth—and converts—these lands would one day bring to the Crown. Even while squarely still lying smack against a continental coast he could conceive of but not recognize, a place he called an "other world," he wrote to his King and Queen: "I desire your Highnesses may be the greatest lords in the world, lords of it all I say, and that all be with much service to and satisfaction of the Holy Trinity."

As the Gulf of Paría narrowed, Columbus sent off his smallest ship to investigate farther west. With her return he learned land closed off passage, and just as he did in western Cuba, he stopped a few miles short of a discovery that might have shown him the truth. Instead, vexed over having to turn back, he came about and headed once more for the strait he would name Mouths of the Dragon.

three

Even today passage through the strait between Trinidad and the Paría Peninsula of Venezuela requires good seamanship and a little nerve. Without any knowledge of the undercurrents that clash there with tides to create a havoc of waters, Columbus entered that egress to the Caribbean. He may have discounted his own maritime capacities too much by crediting only his Providence for bringing the little vessels securely through the Dragon.

Once beyond, he set out on a long northwesterly course that gradually took him away from the peninsula and gave him time to consider whether the coast lying off to the southwest might be not an island at all but a mainland. The length of the shoreline and the vast quantity of fresh water the rivers were pouring out betokened a huge landmass filling them. He recalled some of his ancient texts supporting what he was seeing, and soon after leaving the Dragon he does nothing else than write in his logbook, "I believe that this is a very great continent, which until today has been unknown." Not unknown, of course, to a million or more native peoples.

Remembering the beauty of the landscapes, the fruitfulness of the soil, the moderate climate, and then piecing those things together with legend and myth, sources both classical and biblical, Columbus concluded, astoundingly, that somewhere in this "other world" was the Garden of Eden. For him it all fit, and even his coming upon a continent unknown to Europeans still did not dissuade him from believing he was in the Far East. As he figured it, this "other world" lay somewhere south of China.

Partly because of the necessity of getting supplies and support to his brothers on Hispaniola, the fleet sailed on past the rich pearl beds the Venezuelan Indians had told him about. His former conquistadorial lieutenant Alonso de Hojeda, with the help of an appropriated copy of the Admiral's chart, would find the beds several months later, a discovery that forced Columbus to face untrue accusations that he withheld knowledge of the valuable oysters for his own gain. While he understood that returning to Ferdinand and Isabella with a couple of casks of pearls could buttress his slipping credibility, he knew Santo Domingo needed him and his ships.

He covered more than seven hundred miles of uncharted Caribbean Sea over a surprisingly direct course for the new post on Hispaniola. The last place Columbus had been able to ascertain his position unequivocally was in the Cape Verde Islands off the coast of Africa, weeks before. Given the crude state of celestial navigation and the extreme difficulty then of establishing accurate longitude, the Admiral's arrival on the last day of August 1498, only a hundred miles west of Santo Domingo, a settlement that did not exist when he left the island almost two years earlier, is further evidence—if any is needed—of his masterful dead reckoning.

Waiting for him there were his brothers, the two men he could trust beyond anyone else, and the day was near when trust would become something he would desperately require. Although needing rest and recuperation, he had once again done well on the seas, less so in his land explorations, but he was not unaware of the potential wealth his findings would bring to a country at that time hardly noted for its riches.

four

Because of a good harbor and surrounding fertile country, Santo Domingo was a far better site than La Isabela. As the new settlement went up under the direction of Bartholomew Columbus, relations with the Indians held steady for a while, but things among the Spaniards themselves deteriorated. The man the Admiral had appointed in 1496 to be chief justice, Francisco Roldán, fomented rebellion, not a difficult thing to do among a bunch of toughs who had come to Hispaniola in quest of fast wealth and defilement of Taino women. Roldán calculated that the reports returning to Spain would cause the Sovereigns to rescind powers they had conferred upon Columbus, thereby opening the way for a new governor of the island.

Bartholomew had managed to keep Roldán out of Santo Domingo but did not stop him from roving the countryside; when the three resupply ships that sailed just before the Admiral's departure on the Third Voyage arrived with word that he still enjoyed royal support, the rebel and about seventy men retreated to the far southwest of Hispaniola and made allies of Indians there. Bartholomew answered with a western expedition that subdued native unrest in the area by burning villages, but he made no progress against Roldán. When Columbus arrived on Hispaniola in August, he found his brothers in uneasy control, the natives bludgeoned into quiescence, and about a quarter of the Christians in Santo Domingo ill with syphilis in its secondary stage.

After the supply ships the Admiral had sent ahead from his group at the Canaries finally found Hispaniola, they happened to fetch up near Roldán's position, a bad turn of luck for Columbus. The rebel had little trouble bringing to his camp some of those Spaniards who included the remitted criminals, and he prepared to move against the fortress at Santo Domingo.

The Admiral—and Governor—hurriedly dispatched two of his exploration vessels back to Spain with a report of his findings on the María Peninsula and also a request for reliable and hard-working colonists to replace the malcontents at the fort and to establish an outpost on the Venezuelan peninsula; he also wanted a qualified and honest man to adjudicate issues. He then sent a message asking Roldán to come forth and talk peace. When the leaders met in November, they put together an agreement giving the rebels a choice of ceasing their resistance or returning to Spain with their gold and slaves inside of seven weeks. Later, when Columbus found he was unable to satisfy those terms, Roldán's demands increased to include restoring his position as chief justice, dropping all allegations against him, and—for his followers who wanted them—the granting of western lands along with the foreigners' right to do as they pleased on their holdings and the natives living there. Throughout his dealings with Roldán, Columbus had never dealt forcefully, probably because of his own weakened position, nor did he show strength then by agreeing to the ultimatums as did also the impotent Haitian caciques. The economic provisions granted to Roldán had the horrendous effect of formally creating a system of profiteering that marked early Hispanic history throughout the Western Hemisphere.

In answer to the Admiral's request for a proper judge, the Crown sent out a man of presumed honesty, Francisco de Bobadilla, with power over Columbus and orders to investigate charges of misgovernnance. Directly upon his arrival in August 1500, two years after Columbus had returned to Hispaniola, the royal adjudicator discovered a gallows and seven once rebellious Spaniards hanging from it, with five more to be strung up the next day. The Columbus brothers had finally begun acting potently against other Europeans, but it was too late.

Bobadilla immediately took command by winning over the colonists with a reduced tax on gold. He put Diego Columbus in jail and ordered the Admiral to return from the field to face investigation. When Columbus appeared, the royal adjudicator had him manacled and fettered and locked up. Bartholomew was also upcountry, with a force that probably could have overcome Bobadilla, but his brother told him to cooperate and trust to royal justice, and upon his return he was imprisoned aboard one of the caravels.

In early October, the three men were sent to Spain for trial. Once at sea, the ship captain told the Admiral he would free him from his irons, but Columbus declined, insisting that only the King and Queen could relieve him of them. Once at sea, there was no need, of course, for Bobadilla's enchainment of Christopher, a humiliation endurable only through his belief that these tribulations were either a trial or punishment by his Providence.

There's little question that the Columbus brothers had governed the dangerous, rapacious colony poorly, but whether anyone else could then have managed more effectively so many greedy and barbarous men seeking quick riches by any means, no matter the human cost, is doubtful. Other European nations later would do scarcely better in their first attempts at New World colonies. Far more to the disgrace of Columbus was his ignoring Isabella's disapproval of the slave trade and his establishing an economic system of ruthless exploitation.

And so the Admiral, in bondage, made his sixth crossing of his Ocean Sea, this time in the manner of the hundreds of Indian captives he'd sent over it.

The Fourth Voyage

one

The Admiral arrived at Cadiz toward the end of October. In chains and with a watchful guard, he went on to Seville to stay at a monastery where he had to rely on charity for his keep. Six weeks later Ferdinand and Isabella finally sent money and called him to court. In mid-December, the three Columbus brothers appeared before the King and Queen, and Christopher emotionally presented his account of the Third Voyage and his sufferings so well that the Sovereigns reinstated his stipend and formal titles, although he lost all rights to govern. Las Casas says, "The Queen in particular consoled him, for in truth she more than the King ever favored and defended him, and so the Admiral trusted especially in her." His sons, now Isabella's pages, probably helped keep their father from falling too far from royal grace.

During subsequent months, to assist approval for a

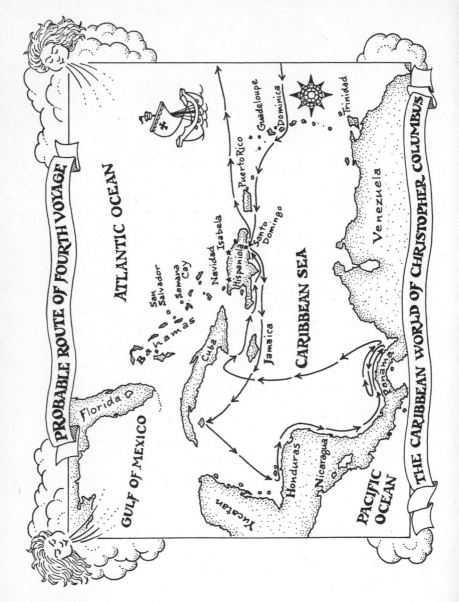

PROBABLE ROUTE OF FOURTH VOYAGE

THE CARIBBEAN WORLD OF CHRISTOPHER COLUMBUS

ATLANTIC OCEAN

GULF OF MEXICO

CARIBBEAN SEA

PACIFIC OCEAN

San Salvador

Samana Cay

Bahamas

Navidad

Isabela

Hispaniola

Santo Domingo

Puerto Rico

Guadeloupe

Dominica

Trinidad

Venezuela

Cuba

Jamaica

Florida

Yucatan

Honduras

Nicaragua

Panama

Fourth Voyage, Columbus and a cleric worked on his *Book of Prophecies,* a compendium of ancient references that he interpreted as forecasts of finding a new world. More practically important to him was another compilation, this one contracts and letters manifesting his rights and titles, that would eventually allow his heirs to make claims against the Crown. He called it his *Book of Privileges.* While he read and copied, other explorers were on the sea to follow routes he'd pioneered and to turn profits from information he provided, a situation that must have galled him. Pressing his requests as best he could, Columbus succeeded in getting the Crown to order Bobadilla in Hispaniola to give an account of the Admiral's holdings there, and the Sovereigns allowed a surrogate of Columbus to sail to the island and return with enough money to keep Christopher affluent the rest of his life.

In early 1502 he began pushing for a new expedition, one he called the High Voyage, into the western Caribbean to search for the presumed strait to India that would open the way to his circumnavigation of the globe. In March, Ferdinand and Isabella granted both permission and underwriting for a Fourth Voyage to gather more geographical knowledge and collect precious metals and stones and valuable spices. But the Queen attached a proviso: There was to be no slaving.

Once again, the resilient and patient Columbus, a foreigner, had prevailed to such a degree that he was even able to draw up letters testamentary to provide for his family, including the unwed mother of his second son.

On the eleventh of May, 1502, a fleet of four caravels, (which the Admiral himself had to pay for), carrying a complement of 140 seamen, many of whom were teenage boys—but no colonists this time—prepared to leave from Cadiz. The captain of one vessel, Pedro de Terreros, had sailed on each of the three previous explorations. Also with Columbus was his younger son, thirteen-year-old Ferdinand, and on another vessel, his reliable but now less-than-eager brother Bartholomew.

The crossing took a mere three weeks. After several stops in the Lesser Antilles, the fleet reached Santo Domingo despite his Sovereigns telling Columbus to stay away from it until his voyage homeward, a prohibition he ignored when he saw signs of a severe storm building. Asking for permission to anchor, the weather-wise mariner alerted Nicolás de Ovando, the new governor of Hispaniola, of the threat, but Ovando laughed at such a "soothsayer" and even denied Columbus safe harbor before sending off his own fleet of thirty ships transporting much royal gold. They were hardly two hundred miles en route when the hurricane caught up. More than five hundred people died, including the Admiral's adversary, Francisco Bobadilla. Only a few vessels survived, including one considered inferior: because of its poor condition, Ovando had assigned to it the agent of Columbus carrying the Admiral's gold. Columbian luck seemed to have returned. As for his own small fleet,

Columbus led it on down the coast a short way to a location where the vessels rode out the hurricane that leveled wood-and-thatch Santo Domingo.

By the end of July, his ships were near the coast of Honduras. Bartholomew took a small crew ashore on a high island, today called Guanaja, but found little except a few natives who wanted to trade *for* the gold and pearls the Spaniards displayed by way of asking where they might find more such goods. Before sailing off, the seamen watched the approach of a gigantic dugout big enough to hold a cabinlike canopy. The Admiral gave orders to seize the canoe and the twenty-five passengers, including women and children, and he permitted his men to steal whatever the Christians wanted; to serve his own mission he impressed an elderly fellow to serve as interpreter. These people appeared more advanced than the island natives: They wore cotton of a sophisticated weave, carried metal axes and swords edged with flint, and in the dugout were crucibles for melting copper. But it was something small and seemingly insignificant they placed the highest value on. For those Indians and others living along the isthmus, cacao beans were their medium of exchange.

Columbus surmised the mythical passage to India must lie to the south, so instead of sailing on west where he would have come into the country of the fallen cities of Yucatán and neighboring regions with their hidden treasures, he turned southeast and headed down along the Mosquito Coast, another poor decision but one that protected Mexican Indians from Spaniards for a few more years. He stopped near the present town of Trujillo, Honduras, and there on August 14, 1502, he at last set foot on the American continent and staked Castilian claim—again, to what he did not know. He was probably the first European to do so in that area but not the first in Central America. Natives by the score appeared on the beach to watch the ceremony. Painted red and black or tattooed with animal designs, these people were eager to engage in vigorous bartering and offered gifts of fish and fowl, beans and fruits. The Admiral's introduction to the great northern continent went well until he began an eastward coasting.

For almost a month, the ships faced hard, opposing winds and weather broken out of some sodden hell. About that leg of the Fourth Voyage, we have the Admiral's own words (here in the colloquial translation of Samuel Eliot Morison):

It was one continual rain, thunder, and lightning. The ships lay exposed to the weather, with sails torn, and anchors, rigging, cables, boats, and many of the stores lost; the people exhausted and so down in the mouth that they were all the time making vows to be good, to go on pilgrimages and all that; yea, even hearing one another's confessions! Other tempests I have seen, but none that lasted so long or so grim as this. Many old hands whom we looked on as stout fellows lost their courage. What griped me most were the sufferings of my son; to think that so young a lad, only thirteen, should go through so much. But Our Lord lent him such courage that he even heartened the rest, and he worked as though he had been to sea all of a long life. That comforted me. I was sick and many times lay at death's door, but gave orders from a dog-house that the people clapped together for me on the poop deck. My brother was in the worst of the ships, the cranky one, and I felt terribly having persuaded him to come against his will.

During those twenty-eight days, the flotilla gained only about 165 miles, and it wasn't until Columbus reached Cape Gracias á Dios—named by him for their deliverance—that the ships could turn southward and take advantage of the winds to move directly and more readily down along the swampy eastern coast of Nicaragua where they encountered few Indians. On September twenty-fifth, the fleet anchored for ten days behind an island near what is today Puerto Limon, Costa Rica, and there things turned interesting again.

two

Before the Admiral could grant liberty to his sailors, Indians with cudgels and palm spears came to the water, so he thought it prudent to hold his men on the ships. As he was deciding on what action to take, the natives, Talamancas, began swimming out to the fleet not to fight but to trade cotton cloth and alloy ornaments. Seeing no pure gold among them, Columbus declined to barter or receive gifts, although he did pass the usual baubles to them, presents the Indians left on the shore, perhaps because it was an insult to take without giving something in return. Yet, still desirous of bartering, their leader sent out to the Admiral a pair of girls, the youngest about eight years old, the elder only fourteen. Had such an offering occurred on one of the earlier voyages, the outcome would likely have been dire for the children, but with his own young teenager looking on, Columbus was now a different commander. Ferdinand later would write:

> The damsels showed great courage; for although the Christians were complete strangers to them, they exhibited neither grief nor sorrow, but always looked pleasant and modest; hence they were well treated by the Admiral, who caused them to be clothed and fed, and sent them ashore, where the old man who had delivered them received them back with much satisfaction.

Perhaps because of this unexpected resistance to the tempting nubility, the Talamancas for a while seemed to view the Spaniards as more than human. The next day, Bartholomew, accompanied by the official secretary of the fleet, led a small party to shore to ask questions and record answers of two natives who seemed to be of some standing. Demonstrating an Indian response not uncommon in later years over much of the Americas, the Talamancas became alarmed by the action of the scribe's weirdly scratching quill. Backing away uneasily, they cast into the air a powder—probably ground chile pepper—to exorcise the sorcery of unnatural strangers seemingly too noble to possess sexual desires.

It was a week before Columbus enjoined a scouting party to explore the area; if his delay was one of caution, it was needless, for the Spaniards primarily came upon abundant wildlife—far more than anyone had seen on the islands—and a native funeral. They found few Indians and no hostility. The Admiral had earlier released the first interpreter when the expedition sailed beyond the area of his language, so Columbus had two Talamancas detained and brought to the flagship. In hopes of encouraging their return, fellow tribesmen sent out a couple of wild boars. The peccary aboard the flagship did not take to the Christians and charged anybody who moved, everywhere scattering tough seamen. To amuse his confined men, Columbus ordered a big spider monkey, wounded by one of his hunters and missing a leg, thrown onto the boar. The bleeding, dying monkey wrapped itself around the peccary's head and sank its teeth in until the boar screamed in pain. The Admiral later described the event to the King and Queen as "fine sport."

On the fifth of October, the respite done, Columbus sailed on eastward to the coast of modern Panama, always alert for the strait that would lead him into the Indian Ocean. But each bay, every inlet, led nowhere but to dead ends. When he got to a large embayment today called Chiriqui Lagoon, he thought he'd finally found the legendary passage that would let him sail west to Europe and achieve a renown that would restore his prestige and privileges. But soon after entering, he saw before him the great Cordillera Central. The truth of the topography stood revealed. But all was not disappointment. Almost as if in recompense, he found the fleet left the area of alloy adornments behind and had entered among the Guaymi Indians who wore things of nearly pure gold and, happily for the Admiral, were willing to trade them for brass bells and glass beads.

From the sixth of October until the sixteenth, the seamen enjoyed themselves in the area of the lovely lagoon. It was there Columbus learned that while no sea egress through the mountains existed, a great body of water did indeed lie not far from them, but he was not equipped for a landward mission, and for some reason—some unexplained, incredible reason—he showed no interest in the isthmus or the ocean beyond it. In his customary way, he intellectualized the world into the topography he wanted it to have: Indian names, foods, clothing, ornamentation, even native skin color all gave evidence he forced to match his textual sources to prove he was now on the Malay Peninsula. With the question of sea passage to the Indian Ocean answered, the Admiral ceased looking for it and didn't mention it again during the voyage. Of all the mysteries surrounding Columbus, this one is among the greatest.

The time had come to hunt for gold, and to do that he sailed on down the coast. Along the Gulf of Mosquitos that fronts the eastern edge of a territory the natives called Veragua, he came upon no seaboard settlements, but he did find the Indians themselves, more than a hundred in one location. When the longboats headed for shore, Guaymis charged into the water, waved spears in menace, and amidst horns and drums, made as if to attack, even spitting a vile herb at the sailors who, for once, calmed things without violence to allow a close approach to trade the usual baubles for disks of beaten gold.

The next day another contentious bartering occurred before the fleet sailed on eastward in hopes of finding the source of the gold. With that stretch of the Panamanian coast having no inlets usable as a harbor, the ships had to keep moving until Columbus learned he was getting beyond the gold region. He tried to turn back west just as the rainy season with its strong, westerly winds began and forced him for a week to lie low in a pretty bay he called Puerto Bello. The trade for cotton goods and food was satisfactory, but the Indians offered no precious treasure.

On the ninth of November, instead of struggling against the wind, the Admiral reluctantly continued eastward, stopping here and there, stumbling into another skirmish with Indians, and accomplishing little more than seriously wearing down the crews and their ships. After a month of that, he decided to turn around to face the winds and fight his way back to Veragua in further search of golden earth, but weather and sea beat the fleet pitilessly, and Columbus went effectively nowhere. We have his own description of those days:

> The tempest arose and wearied me so that I knew not where to turn; my old wound opened up, and for nine days I was as lost without hope of life; eyes never beheld the sea so high, angry and covered with foam. The wind not only prevented our progress but offered no opportunity to run behind any headland for shelter; hence we were forced to keep out in this bloody ocean seething like a pot on a hot fire. Never did the sky look more terrible; for one whole day and night it blazed like a furnace, and the lightning broke forth with such violence that each time I wondered if it had carried off my spars and sails; the flashes came with such fury and frightfulness that we all thought the ships would be blasted. All this time the water never ceased to fall

from the sky; I don't say it rained, because it was like another deluge. The people were so worn out that they longed for death to end their dreadful suffering.

There was yet more to afflict them. Ferdinand Columbus says:

With the heat and dampness, our ship biscuit had become so wormy that, God help me, I saw many who waited for darkness to eat the porridge made of it, that they might not see the maggots; and others were so used to eating them that they didn't even trouble to pick them out, because they might lose their supper had they been so nice.

A kind of relief came in a peculiar form for a couple of calm days when sharks, as if smelling impending death, began circling the ships. Sailors killed the fish for food and distraction, and in this manner the expedition creepingly labored back toward the pleasant lagoon the fleet had left two months earlier.

In late December the Christians again reached the large inlet now known as Limón Bay, the eastern end of the Panama Canal. The exhausted Columbus spent the day after Christmas and the first three days of 1503 less than fifty miles from the Pacific and the sea route to the true Indies that he'd given his life to finding.

three

During January 1503, the rain on the coast of Panama was virtually ceaseless, and almost as disheartening, the Guaymis at first showed small inclination to engage in trading. The flotilla moved on westward to an estuary behind a large sandbar where it stayed put for exploration and minor ship repairs, the best the men could do under the conditions. In early February, a scouting party succeeded in finding a locale upcountry with an exposed gold deposit, enough for Columbus to conclude he should build a fort by the estuary; while Bartholomew oversaw things there, the Admiral planned to go back to Spain for supplies. Things looked auspicious when further explorings turned up other Indians willing to part with their neck disks of gold.

As soon as the crude post—named by Columbus Santa María de Belen—went up, the rain stopped and the river dropped fast, trapping the ships inside the bar. Abruptly prayers changed from "No more rain!" to "Grant us rain!" But of greater danger to the foreigners was the consequence of Christians slipping off to force gold—and, likely, sexual gifts—from the Guaymis. When the Indians realized the fort indicated the intruders were intending to stay, they gathered nearby in large numbers and gave signs they were about to correct an intolerable menace.

The outnumbered Europeans slipped into the interior and managed to capture a cacique named Quibian along with his kin, women and children included, and took them with some plunder back to imprison them on the ships. But before he could be locked up, Quibian jumped into the river and made his way into the forest where he began assembling several hundred warriors. As he did, the rain came on again, the river rose, and the mariners got across the bar all the ships except one they were leaving at the post, and they began preparing for return to Spain and setting up the garrison for the months ahead. Toward the end of the first week of April, on the very day seamen were saying farewell, the Guaymis attacked. For three hours the fight went on with no outcome but injury and death on each side. During it all, Columbus was aboard his ship anchored beyond the river, but he was wracked by a fever and was hearing the voice, so he reports, of his God praising the Admiral's great accomplishments while the man could only weep for all his transgressions.

Over the next few days the fighting came to an end and the Indians withdrew, but the Guaymis captured earlier in the upcountry raid and imprisoned on a caravel decided to resist. At night several of them forced open a hatch and leaped overboard and swam to shore; the ones who didn't make it took a different action. Morison describes it graphically:

When [the hatch] was removed at daylight to give the other captives air, a ghastly sight met the

seamen's eyes. During the night these poor
wretches, some of them women, had collected ropes
in the hold and hanged themselves to the deck
beams, courageously bending their knees while they
strangled, as there was insufficient headroom for a
proper straight-legged hanging.

As the Admiral's fever passed and his mind cleared, he
determined that holding the post, where Bartholomew
was still trapped, would be impossible. His Enterprise
couldn't stand another La Navidad. During the next two
days, his men were able to raft the post survivors and
their stores across the river bar and to the safety of the
three caravels. The stranded ship had to be abandoned.
On the sixteenth of April, the fleet, short of food, set sail
for Hispaniola in a trio of vessels with hulls severely bored
through by shipworms, and the strength and pluck of the
mariners similarly eaten away. Pilots and sailors began
immediately to disagree with their Commander on the
proper course for Santo Domingo, so that he, out-
weighed by a potentially mutinous crew, had to modify
his route to keep things under control.

The ships required bailing with pumps and pails day
and night, an onerous task seamen loathe even for an
hour. And still, one vessel no longer seaworthy had to be
ditched. For the next couple of months the remaining
two caravels, now more sponge than ship, struggled
against wind and currents as their crews did against

hunger and sinking morale, all the while watching the losing battle with intruding seawater. On June twenty-fifth, having sailed as far as he could, Columbus ordered the ships to drop anchor off the north shore of Jamaica near what is today St. Ann's Bay. He called it Puerto Santa Gloria, a name of hope rather than accuracy. The men unloaded supplies and anything else heavy onto a raft and moved it all to the beach before going below into the foul and watery holds to pass up stone ballast and throw it overboard to reduce the draft of the vessels. Then, with all hands bailing madly or turning the windlass to winch each ship landward or leaning into the long oars, sailors ran the caravels, one after the other, into a shallows protected by coral reefs. By getting the worm-riddled hulls alongside to support each other and with timbers to shore them up, the seamen turned two ocean-going ships into stable platforms upon which to build huts of palm. The High Voyage was marooned.

four

Beyond the worries and miseries created by the marooning, Columbus must have found a bit of relief in being back among the Tainos, despite some of the Jamaican tribes offering uncordial receptions on his Second Voyage. Had the grounded ships, regardless of their defensive positioning, been sitting somewhere along the coast of the isthmus, the Spaniards' predicament would have been far worse, probably deadly. As it was, the major immediate and continuing concern was enough food for more than a hundred men who were now out of provisions. To the benefit of both Europeans and Indians, the Jamaican Tainos had no gold or alloy to cause difficulties, but they did have women who went about, when attired, in nothing more than a single patch of centrally placed cotton. The Admiral, knowing the dangerous proclivities of his mariners, most in the full vigor of early manhood, gave orders that no one was to leave the ships without permission. He had learned even the usually complaisant Tainos could be provoked into avenging an abuse.

Diego Méndez, rescuer of the seamen trapped in the post in Panama, volunteered to go into the interior to try to set up trade. A man who never failed Columbus, he succeeded. For beads and bells, the marooned seamen received casava bread, fruits, fish, and meat from muskrat-like rodents called hutias. Soon Tainos from several other places were bringing in food, but Columbus foresaw the demand for cheap European trifles could not last too long. And how long could 116 cooped-up men never noted for civility stay out of trouble? The Admiral knew they all were on borrowed time.

The last longboat had been lost after leaving Panama, and nowhere on the caravels were there proper tools for building even a small craft that could cross the 105 miles from the eastern end of Jamaica to the nearest landfall on Hispaniola. (The total distance from Puerto Santa Gloria to Santo Domingo is about five hundred miles.) Because Jamaica was goldless, no other Spanish explorers had interest in the place, and the possibility of signaling a passing ship was none. The dismal situation on the small, cramped decks was nearly untenable, and it wasn't likely to change soon.

The single hope was a Taino dugout. Once again the bold and resourceful Méndez, whose contributions to Spanish survival all along the way were equal to the Admiral's, went off and managed to trade a brass helmet and some clothing for a good dugout that he modified with a keel and a small sail. On the seventh of July as Méndez made ready, Columbus wrote a hurried and occasionally incoherent letter to his Sovereigns; his debilities may explain his enfeebled self-pity:

> I have no hair upon me that is not white, and my body is infirm and exhausted. All that was left to me and to my brothers has been taken away and sold, even to the cloak that I wore, to my great dishonor. It is believed that this was not done by your royal command. The restitution of my honor and losses, and the punishment of those who have inflicted them, of those who plundered me of my pearls, and who have disparaged my admiral's privileges, will redound to the honor of your royal dignity. . . . Hitherto I have wept for others; now have pity upon me, Heaven, and weep for me, earth! . . .

Isolated in this pain, infirm, daily expecting death, surrounded by a million savages full of cruelty . . . how neglected will be this soul if here it part from the body. Weep for me, whoever has charity, truth, and justice.

This letter does not belong among the finest hours of Columbus, and could the natives have read it, they might have hooted with laughter or cheered such apparent retribution. Across the Caribbean islands, "savages full of cruelty" had often kept the Admiral and his men alive. As for dishonor, plunder, and daily expectation of death, the Tainos understood something about those, just as they understood for whom the earth truly might weep.

Méndez's initial attempt to cross the passage failed. On his next try he took along a second dugout he'd come up with, both canoes carrying seven Christians and ten Indians to paddle. After twenty-four hours, the hard-working Tainos had exhausted their drinking water and were starting to collapse. Before that nightfall, one of them died and the others could no longer sit up. The misery of a slow and risky crossing in the confinement of canoes can only be imagined, and the anguish went on until the morning of the fourth day when the dugouts finally reached an islet that held enough stale water in the hollows of rocks and yielded sufficient shellfish to revive the survivors and allow them to paddle the last thirty miles to the western cape of Hispaniola. There they rested for two days.

Finding six fresh Tainos to work, Méndez moved on along the south shore of Hispaniola but had not gone far when he learned that Governor Nicolás de Ovando, who had denied the Admiral safe harbor from the hurricane, was now punishing Indians in the west. Méndez left the dugout, hiked off inland, and found the bloody governor "pacifying" the Tainos by burning alive leaders or hanging them, not excluding at least one woman. This slaughterous man had no interest in rescuing Columbus and his mariners, so he detained Méndez for half a year before allowing him to walk on to Santo Domingo where there was only a single ship which, of course, wasn't available for rescue. Méndez, apparently prevented or unable to get another dugout, could only sit and wait for a vessel from Spain. Whether his marooned crewmates were still alive, he had no idea.

five

Weeks, then months wore on at Santa Gloria—as unfitting a name as Columbus bestowed—and the marooned men increasingly doubted rescue would ever arrive. Their restricted movements, the cramped quarters, a diet of limited variety (though healthful), and the consequent frictions, all these distresses, topped by an ailing

Commander whose leadership they were now questioning, were classic components of mutiny.

And mutiny there was, instigated by two brothers, Francisco and Diego de Porras, both of whom joined the exploration only through the influence of political connections; knowing nothing of the sea or ships, they couldn't accept the necessity for grounding the sinking caravels. Instead, they spread a rumor that the Admiral was keeping everybody in Santa Gloria because he wasn't allowed to enter Santo Domingo. Their ideas succeeded in splitting the company in half.

The mutineers made off in ten dugouts they paddled up the coast, robbing Tainos and trying to incite them against Columbus as they traveled. Some days later, soon after pushing off for Hispaniola, the sea turned rough and threatened to swamp the canoes. The Christians began throwing Indian paddlers overboard and chopping off any hands trying to hold on. During the month following, the mutineers attempted to cross twice more but succeeded no better. At last the pirates gave up and made a pillaging trek back to Santa Gloria, but they didn't stay; their game was looting.

By early 1504, the molested natives had all the European trinkets they wanted, and bartering declined. Food again became a deep worry. Having virtually nothing material left he could safely offer, Columbus once more showed his resourcefulness, aided immensely and coincidentally by celestial power of a different sort. Among the very few books he carried was an almanac useful to navigators. Bereft of useful goods, about to face starvation, he turned knowledge into salvation, or so says one story.

On February twenty-ninth, he assembled Taino leaders aboard a caravel now sunk securely into the sand, and spoke of his Omnipotence in the Skies and how it had noticed the decline in food being brought to the Christians. On that very evening, at moonrise, the Great Empyrean Cacique would show a sign of celestial displeasure by turning the moon blood red before extinguishing it. The natives were unconvinced. Ferdinand Columbus, who was there, gives this account:

> The eclipse beginning at the rising of the moon, and augmenting as she ascended, the Indians took heed, and were so frightened that with great howling and lamentation they came running from every direction to the ships, laden with provisions, praying the Admiral to intercede by all means with God on their behalf; that he might not visit his wrath upon them, promising for the future diligently to furnish all that they stood in need of. To this the Admiral replied that he wished to converse somewhat with God, and retired while the eclipse lasted, they all the while crying out to him to aid them. And when the Admiral observed that the totality of the eclipse was finished and that the moon would soon shine forth, he issued from his cabin, saying that he had

supplicated his God and made prayers for them, and had promised Him in their names that henceforth they would be good and use the Christians well, fetching them provisions and necessary things. . . . From that time forward they always took care to provide what [the Christians] had need of.

We today can doubt whether Tainos never before had seen a lunar eclipse, but nonetheless, that's the way the son of Columbus recorded a decisive moment of the High Voyage.

And so the Christians continued, endured, clinging to an ever-weakening hope they would find rescue. But rescue, even their sagacious Admiral who had saved them several times was no longer able to bring about. The mariners could rely only on Taino generosity perhaps driven by an eclipse.

six

For a few hours one day in the early spring of 1504, rescue seemed at hand when a small ship sailed around the reefs and dropped anchor near the decaying, wormy hulks, the last remnants of the High Voyage. Her captain, another opponent of the Admiral, paid a visit to him and unloaded salted meat and two casks of wine, gifts from Governor Ovando who had dispatched the vessel not to save Columbus and his men but to check on their survival. A dead Admiral would open the Viceroyalty of the Indies to him. The ship captain passed word that Diego Méndez had indeed made it to Santo Domingo and was waiting for some craft he could charter to send to Santa Gloria. Denied immediate rescue, the marooned mariners at least had their hopes revived by knowing Ovando was aware of their predicament, and Columbus was able to write a letter of thanks to him; diplomacy was by then his sole resource to encourage deliverance.

Wanting to work out a truce, he sent some of the meat to the pirate camp in the bush, but the Porras brothers interpreted the gift as a sign of weakness and decided to attack the grounded caravels. With Bartholomew leading the way against the insurgents, the two groups of Christians set upon each other with swords, while Tainos watched a scene that, at the least, fascinated them and probably gave them considerable satisfaction. Bartholomew and the loyal sailors prevailed and put Francisco Porras in irons. The others Columbus pardoned. How long he could hold together such a patched-up rift he had no idea, but he knew Ovando might effect the Admiral's demise after all.

In the last days of June, a little ship sent by Méndez, who had gone on to Spain to give news of the expedition, reached the stranded men a year after they grounded the sinking caravels. Because the rescue vessel was in sorry fashion and had to fight wind and current, the voyage to Santo Domingo required more than six weeks, but even that was better than life aboard the stinking and rotting caravels. Ovando made a show of receiving the Admiral but released the Porras brothers who escaped punishment altogether, one of them eventually working for the Crown in Jamaica.

On September twelfth, one month shy of twelve years after his initial landfall on Guanahani, Columbus, with Ferdinand and Bartholomew and a few others, boarded a ship he hired to take them to Spain. The crossing took fifty-six trying days. On the seventh of November, 1504, Columbus arrived in the estuary of the tidal river below Seville. The final expedition, the High Voyage that produced more adventure than anything the Crown could immediately respect, was done, and nearly so was the Admiral's health.

He spent the next year and a half, the last days of his life, doing his concerted best to have restored all his privileges and pecuniary perquisites, despite the considerable income his explorations and investments were bringing him. He also, to his credit, did what he could to see that his loyal mariners received proper compensation. But his great supporter, Isabella, died less than three weeks after his return to Spain, and the King, never his reliable advocate, paid him small notice, granting Columbus almost nothing.

Rather than devoting his final months and diminishing energy to penning self-justifying and beseeching letters, had Columbus written a grand and organized account of his four voyages, his name would stand ever higher today, and perhaps it even would have been attached to the two continents now bearing the name of an acquaintance who wrote—or, *had* written—an account of his own travels in the Western Hemisphere that many historians today believe is heavily falsified. But Amerigo Vespucci's *Mundus Novus,* which appeared the year of the Admiral's return, did not fabricate four things: Vespucci (or a surrogate) wrote that a landmass unknown in the Eastern Hemisphere lay westward between Europe and Asia and to reach the Indies by that route a ship had to cross two oceans, not one. He stated with considerable accuracy where that land was, and by skillful celestial navigation he was able to calculate within fifty miles the true circumference of the earth. Amerigo knew how far the East Indies were from the West Indies.

The obdurateness of Columbus, as great a strength as it was a weakness, prevented him to the end from correctly interpreting many facts of his explorations that should have revealed to him where he actually had traveled. He was a man who could only conclude what he wanted to conclude. When he died on May 20, 1506, in his fifty-fifth year, family and friends at his side, he departed on his last voyage still fully believing he had gone where he had not gone and done what he had not done.

He had not sailed to the East Indies, he had not reached Japan or China, he had not found the mythical strait to the Indian Ocean. In his lifetime, his expeditions did not lead to the conversion of more than a few Indians, and the wealth his expeditions eventually brought to Spain did not lead to Jerusalem returning to Christian hands. He had missed being the European discoverer of the Pacific Ocean, had missed becoming the first certain European to set foot on what would become the mightiest nation in the world, and he failed to recognize most of the products beyond gold and silver that would enrich Europe and the Americas and give great import to what he did find.

Yet these failings don't really diminish the great genitor's name. What does detract from his achievements is his establishing practices and reinforcing attitudes that would lead to the extermination of cultures and peoples, perhaps as many as forty million. Judgment of Columbus cannot ignore the forces his actions set in motion in his "other world" that would lead to the greatest genocide humanity has ever witnessed.

Nevertheless, he accomplished what no one before him had: He found a route to open permanently the West to the East, and he initiated the great "Columbian Exchange" of foods, technologies, arts, ways of thought. In doing so, he left a name more recognized—if not always honored—than almost any other in history, and his achievements allowed him to die a comparatively wealthy man. There is no reason, earth, to weep for Christopher Columbus.

A Chronology of
Christopher Columbus

1451	Born in late summer or early fall.
1474	Begins sailing Mediterranean and Eastern Atlantic.
1479	Marries in Lisbon; wife dies six years later.
1480	Son Diego born.
1484	Portugal turns down his Enterprise of the Indies.
1486	Spain rejects his Enterprise.
1487	Spain rejects Enterprise for second time.
1488	Son Ferdinand born.
1492	April 17, Spain agrees to Enterprise.
	August 3, First Expedition leaves Spain.
	October 12, Makes first landfall in the Bahamas.
1493	January 4, Departs Hispaniola.
	March 15, Arrives in Spain.
	September 25, Second Expedition leaves Spain.
	November 3, Arrives at Dominica in Lesser Antilles.
1496	March 10, Departs Hispaniola.
	June 11, Arrives in Spain.
1498	May 30, Third Expedition leaves Spain.
	July 31, Arrives at Trinidad in Lesser Antilles.
1500	October __, Departs Hispaniola.
	November __, Arrives in Spain.
1502	May 11, Fourth Expedition leaves Spain.
	June 29, Arrives in Hispaniola.
1504	September 12, Departs Hispaniola.
	November 7, Arrives in Spain.
1506	May 20, Dies in Valladolid.

Acknowledgments

My thanks to Missourians Mary Barile, Jack LaZebnik, Larry Brown, and JoAnn Graveman for their special and generous help. In New York I am grateful to Hana Lane, Pamela LaBarbiera, and Lois Wallace. In Florida, Marvin Lunenfeld.

Of the several prominent studies of Christopher Columbus, most of them unhappily no longer in print, I owe particular debt to naval historian Samuel Eliot Morison for his splendid two-volume biography, *Admiral of the Ocean Sea: A Life of Christopher Columbus* (1942). Morison tells the story of the great Genoese navigator from the point of view of a blue-water sailor that Morison himself was. His *Journals and Other Documents on the Life and Voyages of Christopher Columbus* (1963) contains much key secondary material from the fifteenth and sixteenth centuries, including his translation of the logbook of the First Voyage. For a more recent version of that journal, I also used *The Diario of Christopher Columbus's First Voyage to America* (1989), by Oliver Dunn and James E. Kelley Jr. I felt free to quote from both translations, choosing whichever one I thought expressed a particular passage more clearly or felicitously. Although there still is no complete English translation of it, the revealing and astonishing *History of the Indies* by Bartolomé de Las Casas deserves a much wider audience in America than it has received; the fullest abridgement (1971) is by Andrée Collard.

Recent secondary studies I found especially enlightening are Irving Rouse's *The Tainos: Rise & Decline of the People Who Greeted Columbus* (1992) and David E. Stannard's *American Holocaust: Columbus and the Conquest of the New World* (1992). The bibliography of Columbian studies is voluminous, but these few basic works will serve to get interested readers started on a voyage of their own.